From behind the veil

A HIJABI'S JOURNEY TO HAPPINESS

Farheen Khan

Dear Sabira,
Thank you so much for your
support!

BURMANBOOKS

Published by BurmanBooks Inc.
260 Queens Quay West
Suite 1102
Toronto, Ontario
Canada M5J 2N3

Cover design: Joshi Inc. www.joshiinc.com
Interior design: Jack Steiner Graphic Design
Editing: Drew Tapley

Distribution:
Innovative Logistics LLC
575 Prospect Street, Suite 301
Lakewood, NJ 08701

ISBN: 978-1-897404-23-2

Printed and bound in Canada

Dedication

My family: Baba, Mummy, Badeapa, Afreen, Ayesha, Shoaib, Maryam (Mary), Muzammil (Muzzy), Juwi, Summi and the boys; my best friend Sanjitha and all my other friends (you know who you are) for supporting me throughout my journey, and to all those who have or are suffering from a trial or tribulation today. My thoughts and prayers are with you all.

بسم الله الرحمن الرحيم

"Thank you Allah"

For giving me the strength to endure adversity
while others rest.

For teaching me that patience is a virtue
during all tests.

For sending me a great family and wonderful friends
who have supported me through thick and thin.

For reminding me to keep a positive attitude,
have faith and things will be normal once again.

For making me understand that life isn't always
in our control; and sometimes when things go wrong
it's for a reason that someday we'll know.

For reminding me to appreciate what I have and
to think of them as precious commodities.

For being fortunate for my situation, as there are
others elsewhere in worse difficulties.

For helping me realize that life isn't just about
this world and what you can gain; it's about
remembering you Allah* in happiness and in pain.

---

* Subhana Wa T'ala; meaning: Allah, Glorified and Exalted is He.

Table of Contents

CHAPTER 1

From the Beginning

*"There are many things in life that will catch
your eye, but only a few will catch your heart
... pursue those."*

MICHAEL NOLAN

Key Points

- Standing your ground
- Importance of having a strong foundation
- Follow your intuition
- You're never too young or inexperienced
  to do the right thing

The importance of a strong foundation

We are all affected by life's challenges, but it's how we deal with them that makes us who we are. I believe destiny is the process of bringing a person from one stage to the next, where the next stage far exceeds what they had ever expected. Before I get started with my own journey, I think it's important for you to get to know the person I am. For that, we need to go back to the beginning....

My name is Farheen Khan, and my name means "happiness." I was born in 1980 in the city of Mississauga, Ontario. I am the second of seven children born to my parents Nazir and Noor Khan, who migrated from Hyderabad, India in 1971. I've never been to India, nor have most of my siblings, and since immigrating to Canada my parents have only been back to India a handful of times to see relatives. That being said, my family was mostly born and raised in Canada, yet we follow the traditions of India as best as we can, since we only hear about it through our parents.

Growing up in Mississauga during the 1980s was an interesting experience. I grew up in a semi-conservative household among a very small Muslim community in the Peel region. As far back as I can remember, I recall being with my father, sitting in a lecture or listening to an Imam speaking. This was unlike most other South Asian girls in Canada who spent more time at home with their mothers. Being with my father meant living the life of a tomboy. I lived, breathed and dreamed cars and other boy things, and this set me apart from most of the girls I knew and kept me connected to boys at an early age. Spending time with my father also kept me very close to the mosque and taught me the importance of being the protector and the responsible person in the family.

My father, being the man he is, decided that Mississauga needed a mosque; and so he began his journey of starting the first mosque in Mississauga. During this period, I spent even more time in the mosque with him, and learned about organization and leadership. I realized that I can do and be who I want to be, and that standing your ground and making firm decisions was an important part of a person's life. Yes, I was fairly young when I realized this, but it was definitely a lesson that I carry with me even now.

Childhood sickness and faith healing

From the age of a toddler, I was very sick and constantly in and out of the hospital because of high fevers and convulsions. In the first few years of my life, I spent more time in the hospital than I did at home. My parents were certainly concerned about my health, so were the doctors; but unfortunately no one could figure out what the cause of the convulsions and high fevers was. Now we realize that these reactions occurred after eating certain foods (e.g. spinach, lentils, beans, and peanut butter). I also had a very hard time breathing, which could have been a result of my father's habit of smoking in the home (but that's debatable).

Because of my constant sickness, my parents started speaking to friends and family about possible healing methods. Through this process, they came across the idea of using faith healing to cure my ailments. The man that my father would take me to was called Abdul Qadir Mehmisani. He was a pious Lebanese man who simply recited words from the Holy Qur'an to heal any ailment a person was experiencing. Having been very young at the time, I vaguely remember him as a very fair-complexioned man with a small white cap on his bald head, clean shaven, and wearing a long white *thobe* (Arab-style robe for men). He would give me candy and I would sit still for at least forty minutes at a time while he recited the verses. I was a four-year-old, and this was not an easy task. If I started fidgeting, he said nothing, but just his look was enough to say "stay in your spot." My father took me back a number of times for healing sessions, and there was a lot of gradual improvement.

To this day, I am very grateful for having met such a pious person. May Allah* grant him *Jannah* (paradise) in the hereafter.

English as a second language

For the most part, when I became school-aged my health was much more in control than before. School was an exciting experience. I was very eager to go to school, unlike some of my kid siblings who were terrified about the idea of leaving my mom. I still remember the first day of kindergarten. My mother was more nervous than I was, and was concerned that I wouldn't be able to handle the separation. But that wasn't the case at all. I was very excited. And so in the morning I got dressed, ate my breakfast, and then walked to school with my mom and sister. When we got to the door, I took one look at my mom and said, "Okay, bye," and walked right in.

I was eager to attend school, but what I didn't realize was the mighty challenge I would have to face from day one. I didn't speak a word of English. So, you can imagine how challenging it must have been for me to communicate with my teacher. Growing up, the rule of our house was no English in the home, and so I was fluent in Urdu only. Embarrassingly enough, even though I was born and raised in Mississauga, I still ended up attending ESL classes (English as a

Second Language) until age ten. Because of the label that "ESL" kids have of being "fresh off the boat," I had few friends in the school. Most of my friends were family friends or kids that I saw at Sunday school or in the evenings at the small Islamic class at my home. Most of my friends were guys, and I rarely spent time with girls—I just couldn't relate to them. My father raised me as a tomboy, and so I was into race cars, transformers and GI Joe; as opposed to my sister who was into Barbie dolls, Lady Lovely Locks and Prince Bride cartoons and toys. My elder sister and I were in the same school for a while, so being the youngest at the time I was spoiled quite a bit. I was a very active kid in school; I joined the soccer team, and loved to pick up lady bugs and worms and run after the boys and girls in my class.

Fasting during the summer months

I first decided to fast during the month of Ramadan when I was six-years-old. I remember being the first person to spot the "new moon" that year from my apartment building. I was awed by the beauty of the new moon, and upon seeing it recited: "La Ilaha Ill Allah Muhammadur Rasool Allah" (there is no God but Allah*, and Muhammad† is the Messenger

---

† Peace be upon Him.

of God). It was at that point that I decided I would keep all thirty fasts that month. If God gave me the privilege of seeing the moon before anyone else, I was definitely going to take the benefit of this and keep all of my fasts.

My parents told me that I wasn't old enough to fast, and that if I wanted to I should wait until the fall or winter fasts began in a few years. I was angered by the fact that they were trying to hold me back from observing the fast, which is one of the five pillars of Islam. So, at age six, I woke up and started fasting on my own. The summer fasts were brutal. We ate breakfast at 3 a.m., and by 7 a.m. when it was time to go to school, the food had already digested. We were literally starving until 9 p.m. that night. I remember coming home from school and sitting at the dining table holding my stomach and crying until it was time to eat.

My mother took a lot of heat from the family about letting me fast, but I was determined to do it. One day she decided not to wake me up and I kept the fast without having *sehri* (breakfast). When I woke up, I told my mom I would do it *"bin sehri"* (without breakfast), and that if she did that to me again she would be punished for holding me back. From that point forward my mom woke me up every day and I completed my thirty days of fasting. During that Ramadan, I also made a point of going to the mosque every night for *Taraweeh* (prayers). My mom was busy at home with the kids, so I went on my own. A lot of "aunties" (my many mothers at the mosque) were always concerned about me, and they watched out for me and made sure I was well taken care of.

The importance of seeking knowledge: My first mentor

One night during Taraweeh at the mosque, I was praying and heard an amazing voice coming from the men's section. It was the new imam my dad had hired from the United Kingdom. He was such an amazing orator, reciting as though he was singing yet so quickly and without any errors. To me, that meant he really knew his stuff, and I was inspired and determined to learn from him. Every night, we had a question and answer session with the imam after prayer. The women, being in a separate room, were supposed to write down their questions and pass them to a volunteer who would take them to the men's side. I wrote in my six-year-old handwriting: "To the new hafiz, I want to learn how to read from you. My name is Farheen. Please speak to me after the prayer." I immediately told my father about what had happened and the decision I had made.

My dad arranged for me to have a phone conversation with him. I told him on the phone that I was interested in learning from him, and that he was the only teacher I wanted to finish the Qur'an with. He was very young at the time himself, probably in his early twenties, and a very nice man. He said that he could teach me, but it would have to be over the phone. To me that wasn't good enough. The phone? How would I learn? I told him that I wanted to learn in person, so he told me to gather some other kids and if there were enough people he would come and teach all of us. I agreed to this, and off I went to recruit as many of my friends as possible to join the class with me.

After three months of convincing, I was able to gather enough kids and we finally got my favourite hafiz of all time to teach me: Hafiz Dawood. He's also the one who inspired me to consider *hifzing* (memorizing the Qur'an), which I still have to complete at some point during my lifetime. Thank you Hafiz Dawood for taking me seriously and helping me finally finish the Qur'an in Grade 6.

Follow your heart: Observing the hijab at age nine

When I turned nine, my father had rented out a small apartment on top of a shop as a place of worship. This was a result of the Islamic class we had in our apartment, which was now so fully occupied in the evenings that we really had no room left to move around. My mother would take me and my elder sister there for a monthly ladies-only lecture. It was a program designed to talk to women about Islam and to help guide them with managing their lives in society, as well as at home. During one particular session, I remember clearly the topic of discussion was about the Hijab—the head scarf that Muslim women wear to cover their hair. The lady who led the session was Aunty Nafisa Khan. To be honest, I can't remember a lot of what she said, just tidbits of information here and there, like the fact that wearing the hijab in this world will be a key to granting you paradise. At that time, the other part that stuck with me, was that in paradise, Allah* will come to see all the women personally that had worn the hijab during their life, for the sacrifices they made. Finally, it is believed that the hijab is a way of protecting women from pre-marital relationships and harm, because it is believed by Muslim scholars that a woman's hair and her eyes are the most beautiful parts of her body and by covering these parts, it's expected that women will not bring attention onto themselves. I'm not a scholar by any stretch of the imagination, but I do remember reading in the Qur'an about this:

O Prophet! Say to your wives and your daughters and the women of the faithful to draw their outer

garments (jilbabs) close around themselves; that is
better that they will be recognized and not annoyed.
And God is ever forgiving, gentle. (SURAH AL-AHZAB
33:59)

There is still some controversy about this verse
because the assumption is that women are being told
to cover their bodies and not their heads. However,
according to other sources like Hadith (scholarly
journals from the time of the prophet Muhammad[†]),
it is understood that women would cover their heads
based on the cultural norms that existed at the time.

As soon as she finished her lecture, I got up and
walked over to my mother and said, "Mummy, starting right now I want to wear the hijab." My mother
was shocked, considering she didn't wear the hijab
herself at the time. On the way home, I kept my scarf
on as we walked back to our apartment building.

Show and tell

My mother was a bit concerned since the Muslim
community was quite small and there was fear of
discrimination to visible minorities. Yet, she could
see that I was determined to wear the hijab. I still
remember the first day that I wore the hijab to school,
and I was really nervous about what the kids would
say. I knew that I had done my due diligence by telling

them all about it, but I was still quite apprehensive. I kept repeating to myself that I'm wearing it for God and he'll protect me, and when I got to school the kids treated me like they usually did. I didn't hear anything at all. It was as though they didn't even see it. Throughout elementary school, the kids weren't too cruel towards me because I had made a point of doing a "show and tell" session with the class in advance, so they understood what I was going to do and why. For the most part, the kids were fine with it. To this day, when I run into people that knew me in elementary school, they don't remember me even wearing the scarf. They say that they were so used to me, it wasn't something important enough to remember. My father was concerned that I was wearing it as well. He didn't think I was old enough to make such a serious decision, but I was certain that the decision I made was a lifelong commitment on my part. He did what he could to keep it very low-key with people at work and in his circle. Being a traffic cop, my dad often had to go to court to challenge a ticket, and as usual when he was going to court, he asked if I wanted to come along.

I used to go to court with him a lot, but when I got into the car with my dad and my sister (both of us were now wearing hijabs) my dad told us to remove the hijabs before going inside. My sister refused and decided to sit in the car until he returned—but me being me—I ran into the hall before my dad could grab my hand. He slowly ran after me, I knew he was furious, but he tried to keep calm, cool and collected in front of his colleagues. When he finally parked the car and came into the foyer, he found me sitting on the lap of one of the other officers, drawing a picture. He was surprised that the response was so positive. They behaved towards me just like they would have with any other child. From that point forward my dad was supportive of my decision.

Adjusting to change as a visible Muslim

When I was in Grade 6, my parents moved to a completely different area of Mississauga. It was here that I experienced first-hand the feelings of discrimination for being a visible Muslim. I was "the only hijabi" in the school. Students made comments about the hijab and started treating me differently from others. Comments such as, "I bet you're bald under there," or "What's that, a pillowcase on your head?" became common. I never did let it get to me, and I did my best to stay calm and carry on with life, but being a teenager who just couldn't fit in was certainly a frustrating issue to deal with. It was a real challenge making friends and trying to get through school while being bullied the way that I was. I remember one time when a Muslim boy came up to me and pulled my scarf back—I was furious! I turned and slapped him really hard across his face. When asked by my teacher why he did this, his only response was that he was curious to see if I had hair under my scarf. Since so many people were convinced that I was bald underneath the scarf, he wanted to prove otherwise to them.

Even though I was so actively involved at school, I felt lonely and like something was missing; a friendly connection that I once had with my elementary friends. I was lucky to meet Reshma in Grade 6. She was new to the country and new to the school, so when I saw her I befriended her. Coincidentally, we turned out to be neighbours too, with our houses facing each other. We became the best of friends in a very short time, and soon after we had a group of about a dozen girls. It was great to see all the diversity of ethnicity and culture in the group, not to mention it was the first time I was hanging out with an all-girl crowd. Let's just say, for the first time in years I was introduced to my feminine side.

Accepting new roles

From a young age, I was always the strong one in my family. My mother is a very soft person and my father a stern and strict person, although in my case he's often soft. I have one elder sister and five younger siblings (three girls and two boys), all of whom are roughly less than fifteen months apart. As a child, my parents gave me everything I wanted, and I was spoiled (see Ayesha, I admitted it!). But that didn't last very long with so many younger siblings around, and I was quick to take on my role as the "eldest" at home. My elder sister married young and left the home quite early, so it was my responsibility to be the elder and more responsible sister. Now being the eldest, I had to start thinking about my siblings. I did what I could to always keep them active, busy and having fun, especially considering my father was always active with the mosque and with work, and he was often tired and unable to take the kids out for leisure and recreational activities. My younger siblings all called me "Apa," which means "big sister" in Urdu. Once they started calling me this outside the house, the rest of the neighbourhood started calling me that too. It got to the point where no one knew my real name. My younger brother Muzammil actually thought that was my name. To me, this meant teaching them all of the things that I had learnt growing up. My dad spent hours with me and my elder sister, and taught us how to swim and ride a bike; so now it was my turn to pass on the knowledge to my younger siblings.

Setting up the Muslim students association at school

In high school, I discovered many things about myself, including the idea of being an example for others, making my own style, being a leader, working for the rights of others, and establishing my own boundaries and guidelines. It was at this time that I also started to develop my dreams and goals for the future. I guess the most significant realization was the idea that I was ready to be a more faith-based and visible Muslim regardless of the norm.

That being said, I was determined to start wearing the *abaya* (a long over-garment that women wear to cover their clothing). Unfortunately, I had gym class in semester one of Grade 9, so it didn't make sense to wear the abaya during school hours if I was going to be participating in gym class. I told my mom that I would start wearing the abaya in semester two, and I did. I saw the difference in the behaviour of some of my friends immediately. It was like there was this wall that was suddenly put between me and them. I was now visibly different and didn't fit into the mold of what a "teenage girl" in high school should look and dress like.

I was always very involved in high school and was a part of many different extracurricular groups, presiding over my school's MSA (Muslim Students

Association) for quite some time. It was quite the challenge to start up a Muslim association without the support of the boys in the school, as none of the Muslim boys chose to come forward. So I did my best to find people to come into the school to do the Friday sermons. I even went out of my way to teach some of the Grade 9 students how to deliver a sermon, and I am no scholar by any account. I already had a much bigger vision for my school's MSA, and I realized that unless I had a male counterpart at the school, I would not be able to work with other MSAs across the city. So I found a boy in the school whom I knew from childhood, but getting him to come to meetings with me and other school heads was like pulling teeth. Even though it was hard work, we made it through the school year and were able to get things done.

The poverty affect

During high school, I had the opportunity to learn first-hand what poverty means and what it feels like to be in a situation where food is no longer a pleasure, but rather a commodity. As a family of nine, with my father as the sole income earner, we were living in subsidized housing. I know my father struggled but he was still able to make ends meat (thanks Baba).

Then one day, to make things worse, a family

situation forced my father to go to India for a few months. He took out a whole bunch of loans to make the trip, and was convinced that for the sake of his family back home that the trip was necessary. He was also sure that when he returned he would work hard for a few months to make up the money he borrowed, and things would be normal once again. My mother, although hesitant about the whole situation, understood and allowed him to go. He was gone for four weeks, which seemed to be the longest four weeks of my life. At the time, I was the eldest child at home, and so I felt like a lot of the responsibility was on me, and I did what I could to help my mom manage the family resources for the next month.

When my father came back, we were all relieved, but he was very ill when he arrived. None of us knew what was happening. My mother rushed him to the hospital, and there we discovered that he had been infected with a deadly case of malaria. By the time he had travelled back to Canada, he had already had it for two days. This particular type of malaria only lasts four days and must be cured quickly otherwise it can cause severe illness, and even death. Our family doctor made regular visits, and after two days, multiple visits, lots of medications and my mom's sincerest *duas* (prayers), my dad overcame the malaria. Unfortunately, this really had taken a toll on his health and he was bedridden for the next six months. You can imagine what that can do to a family's finances—especially to a family of nine.

With my father unable to work, my mother at home with the babies, and me going to high school, we had little money coming in and a lot of expenses to pay back. I still remember the time my mom asked me to go to the store and get some milk for the kids. I had a penny jar which I never thought I'd use, but at that point with nothing left, I literally counted out two hundred and fifty pennies and took them with me to the store across the street. The cashier gave me a hard time but took them in the end. I still remember my brother Shoaib seeing a box of cookies and crying to get it. Unfortunately I had spent all of what I had brought and I knew that my jar was empty at home as well. I still remember how hard it was to reassure the kid that we would come back to get it, knowing that I had no means to give him the $2 box of cookies he wanted.

At that point, I lost it and decided that I would do whatever was needed to keep the family running until my father returned to work. The first thing I did was sell all of my gold jewellery which my mom had collected over the years for my wedding. My mom was unhappy with the fact that I got back far less than she had spent, but to me the fact that this could cover the kid's food expenses for a week was more than enough. Slowly we started selling our furniture and I started tutoring a kid or two after school as well. These were by far the most difficult six months I experienced in high school.

Going through this experience re-emphasized in my mind the importance of excelling in what you do and being ambitious. Until and unless you consciously set goals for yourself, there is very little that will change in your life. I was convinced that I had to give my family and I a much better life than we had experienced over the last year.

CHAPTER 2

Reach for the Stars!

LESSON: Setting Goals, Dreams and Ambitions

*"Reach for the Moon, even if you miss,
you'll land among the stars!"*

LES BROWN

Key Points

- The importance of dreaming, setting goals and being ambitious
- Follow your dreams, anything is possible
- Strategically plan out your future

From a young age we are taught to plan out our life. Whether it is to plan our class timetable or pick our courses in high school to prepare for university and college, we are always taught to have a sense of control on how things will end up. This teaches us that success lies within our reach: Reaching for the stars.

Setting goals is an important part of our lives. Without this process, we really would not know where we're going. In my life, I had lots of plans for where I wanted to go but they seemed to change over time based on circumstances. For the longest time I dreamt about being a doctor. I took all the courses in science and math, but quickly realized that I wasn't as strong in these courses as the arts and English, so I changed my mind and decided to go into English and pursue a degree in teaching or journalism; but even that was not meant to be.

The late American professor of computer science, Randy Pausch, who died of pancreatic cancer in 2008, gave a final lecture—*The Last Lecture*—and wrote a book of the same title about achieving your childhood dreams. If you haven't read his book then definitely take out the time to read it or listen to his lecture on YouTube. Randy is a prime example of a person who had dreams and made many of them a reality, but sometimes the way in which they occurred were very different based on circumstances.

Dreams, goals and achievements

When I left high school, I had every intention of going to university to become an English teacher or even a lawyer so that I could support my family fully, especially after seeing them in the state they were in at the time. I never wanted them to go through what they had experienced a few months earlier, but to get into university I needed money; which unfortunately I didn't have. My father has always been the kind of person to help others, but he never believed in future planning. He was always about doing what he could to help today, even if it was at the expense of his own family's future. Getting a student loan was out of the question because of *ribba* (interest which is forbidden in Islam). I couldn't justify to myself that I would compromise my religious beliefs to take a loan and study in order to better my future, when the future and everything in my life is supposed to be lived for the sake of Allah*. This meant I would have to start working first and then save up enough to go to college or university.

My first experience working was with a temp agency doing light packaging for a hygiene products manufacturer. I figured that it was something temporary that I would do until I was ready to go back to school. Boy, was I wrong! I went there one day and swore that I would never go back. I told my dad, and he told me that the only way to get a decent job would be for me to do some sort of an IT course.

I enrolled in an IT course, and during this course the vice president of an IT firm downtown came to speak to my class. After he spoke, we were given an opportunity to ask questions. No one else in the class said anything, but I did. I asked him, "How am I supposed to get a job when everyone wants job experience and nobody wants to give me a chance to get any experience?" Well, that was the end of that. He hired me right away, and so thankfully I didn't have to go through the whole job search process. I worked at a large health management firm for six months as a junior technical analyst, and was let go soon after along with all of the other Muslim employees. When we asked the reason why, we were told that there had been some fraudulent acts by the employment agency. However, we knew otherwise. If that was the case, then all of the employees hired through the agency would have been fired, right? Wrong! Only those who were visibly Muslim—like me, or who had obvious Muslim names were laid off.

I would now have to compete with others in the market for a job, as a visible Muslim minority. Although diversity and multiculturalism was and is still always encouraged in Canada, there was always a difference between the way we were treated as

Muslims compared to white Caucasians—especially when it came to looking for a job.

After lots of visits to employment agencies, and lots and lots of interviews, I finally landed a job at a Government service provider as a Customer Service Representative. The atmosphere at this place was wonderful, everyone was supportive of each other and people were treated equally. There was no mention about religion, and we all worked in a very positive environment.

Climbing the corporate ladder

After six months of working as a Customer Service Representative in the call centre, I was promoted to Customer Support Specialist where I became a supervisor for other call centre representatives. A few months later, I was promoted again to a Learning Support Analyst, and I had a chance to attend many meetings and work with different people at many levels of the organization.

I made sure that I was always setting an example of what a Muslim was to others, and as long as I was comfortable being myself and doing what I had to do, what other people thought or felt about me didn't matter. This perspective didn't come to me overnight, and in the past I was afraid to do many things because I wasn't sure how people would react.

Now, I was roaming the streets freely without any fear of who I was, and although I still got the same type of stares it no longer concerned me.

One of the reasons for my self-confidence is something that my Grand Uncle Asif Ali shared with me. It was a profound concept that really resonated and stayed with me as a wonderful reminder that doing what I believe in is important, and if I am going to make a point of affecting others through my existence, I must always remember to set a good example. He told me how in the world there are two types of people: dots and stars. The dots are people doing their thing in life; they are generally the same, living life the same way, dressing the same, eating and doing similar things. Stars, on the other hand, are unique and different because they don't follow the norm and they create their own path. As a result, the stars are often the centre of attention. He informed me that I am a star because of the way I dress and the responsibility I have chosen to take on as an individual in society.

He also warned me not to "try acting like dots to fit in, because you're different. Don't try hiding behind a dot because you won't be able to. Just accept that you are a star and the centre of attention in your life. People will always look to you as being an example, and always remember to lead by example and live responsibly, for not just yourself but also for the others that you may influence and affect through your presence."

To this day, I keep this ideal in mind that being and working responsibly and sometimes being the centre of attention can work to my advantage, only if I work and live positively for the benefit of others. Being the centre of attention also has its downside, like being in the public eye without much privacy. But honestly, that's the price one has to pay to do what's needed for a brighter future.

Fulfilling my dreams

My first car was a 1989 grey-blue Honda Accord DX. My father bought it from an auction house for $678, and I remember the look on the man's face at the auto shop when I asked him to paint my grey blue car to an electric blue—or more specifically: "Pearl blue sapphire." It was so me... a little funky, a little original, and something unique that said: "This is Farheen." I loved driving my Honda down the street wearing my sunglasses and listening to my loud music. At first, people started giving me strange looks as to why in the world "a hijabi" who in their eyes was the quiet submissive type—was driving a sports car down the street.

My university tuition was also something my employer agreed to take care of as long as I could study on my own time and it somehow tied into my day-to-day job. I was set. So I decided to pursue my degree at York University in administrative studies with a major in marketing. I had dreams of pursuing my MBA at Schulich School of Business immediately after I graduated from my undergraduate degree.

When I turned twenty-one, I bought my first home. It was an interesting experience being so young and buying something that became a family home, not just my own home. Essentially I bought it for my dad because he was too stubborn to buy an interest-based mortgage on his own. I appreciated his reasoning, but in a world that didn't really have any alternatives I felt it was my role to make a point. That didn't last very long, and after six months of living in a small townhouse (which was the only thing I could afford at the time) my dad went out and bought his own house.

Real control or simply an illusion?

When setting goals, it's always important to keep in mind your ultimate purpose in life. As a Muslim, our ultimate goal is to seek the pleasure of Allah* (God almighty) and to attain jannah (paradise). We often get so caught up with life that we get distracted. I won't say that I was completely distracted, but I definitely got sucked into the materialistic and capitalistic views of the world.

Let's just say that at age twenty-one I had it all. I was on my way to start a very promising career, everything was planned and ready; I had dotted all the I's and crossed all the T's in my life. I was just an ordinary Canadian woman who had a dream of living a financially worry-free life with a large home on the side of the beach and two expensive cars. I spent my week going to work and school, and my weekends spending time with my family.

In the words of the American philosopher and psychologist John Dewey: "Arriving at one goal is the starting point to another." My life was going exactly how I had planned it, but what I didn't realize was that God had a completely different plan for me, which was heading towards me at high speed.

CHAPTER 3

Shattered Dreams

"When it seems that someone has shattered your dreams... pick up even the smallest of pieces and use them to build bigger and better dreams."

UNKNOWN

"A gem is not polished without rubbing, nor a man made perfect without trials."

CHINESE PROVERB

Key Points

- Making sense when things don't go as planned
- Dealing with trials and tribulations

In 2001, I was still working as a Learning Support Analyst. Life was going well for me, and things were exactly as I had planned them to be. I could have lived my whole life exactly as I had planned it, but things don't always work out the way we plan them. Many people have different opinions and thoughts on destiny, but in my mind, destiny is the path that God creates for us. We often think that we have the control, and in some ways we do, but in the grand scheme of things we have little control over a much larger plan that may or may not coincide with our own.

The tragedy of September 11, 2001

Many people will say that 9/11 had an impact on their lives. There are many people who embraced Islam after this time, and many others that felt more comfortable abstaining from sharing their identity. I have talked about this date with a lot of people, and most North Americans remember exactly where they were on that day and what they were doing. Some were affected more than others. In my life, 9/11 played an important role, but in a different way. In one sense, it was the starting point for much of the tribulation I had to go through in my life as a young adult. But it was also a turning point for me; a point of departure for who I am today.

Before this date, I felt safe and felt free to be

myself. After the twin towers fell it seemed as though my efforts to educate individuals in society about the hijab were all in vain. The term "Islamophobia" suddenly emerged out of the air and became common use for at least the next eight years and beyond.

On that horrifying morning, I walked into the office oblivious to what had happened. Everyone there was quiet and listening to the radio. I asked them what had happened and they explained that the twin towers had been destroyed. I couldn't believe my ears! I immediately started to see the change in attitude from people when I went down to the lobby in our building, and to the bank. After seeing the anger and frustration that people had when they looked at me, I started to feel unsafe. When I returned home that evening, I started to see stories on the news of the backlash that was occurring towards the Muslim community.

At this point, I was completely terrified of what was happening. I began to feel as though I was being persecuted by society for my religious beliefs. I know about homophobia, but does the same principle apply to the phobia of a faith? In Islam, growing up, we were taught to condemn the homosexual act and not the individual, but if the same principle applies, then this wasn't the case for Muslims after September 11, 2001 (9/11). Until this point I had always heard about religious persecution and had thanked Allah* that I lived in Canada, in a place where this did not happen. Well I was wrong. I am a Canadian Muslim woman born and raised in Canada, being treated like a foreigner only because I was dressed in a cultural way and followed a religion that is similar to suspected terrorists. How fair is that?

The emergence of Islamophobia

As soon as I heard what had happened, I went home. I remember my director at work asking me if I felt safe enough to walk back to my car, or if I needed an escort. I told her I was fine, and went home. I just needed to think about this clearly. I stayed at home trying to decide whether I was ready to live as a "person of colour" and a Muslim knowing that it could affect my safety and well-being. After a few days of being in total shock, I regained my senses and decided that enough was enough. I had nothing to do with this whole thing, I shouldn't have to hide or be afraid, and I decided to move on with my life. It was a difficult decision but I could not justify to myself that taking off the hijab (which I was wearing for Allah[*]) was the best way to protect myself. However, not all hijabi's made the same decision as me. Some decided that being safe was more important and removed the hijab temporarily; and others permanently. The one thing that I really appreciated during this time was how the Government declared that any backlash against Muslims was against the law. In the past, most of the persecution and discrimination came from the Government with respect to aboriginal and first nations people; so this was definitely an improvement on that front.

Since that day, I have received an increasing number of cold and horrified looks from many people. I have experienced a number of personal incidents by-way of this tide of Islamophobia. Some of these have been more severe than others. I have included in this chapter only some of the experiences that I endured thereafter in my everyday life as a hijabi. Most of these stories are sad, as they show how fear and ignorance about the hijab forces people to do strange things. In some ways they're also very humorous—but it took me a while to think of them in that way.

The grocery store

One day when I was shopping at the local grocery store, a man with a very thick European accent came up to me and said, "Go back to where you came from you freak!" This totally threw me off guard, and I said to him, "What do you mean go back to where I came from? I was born here and have lived here all my life. What about you? Were you born here?" He shook his head to say "no" and then I said, "So how would you like it if I was to do the same to you?" He apologized and went on his way.

The elevator

One evening as I was leaving work, I got into the elevator to go to the lower level where my car was parked. At first, the elevator was completely empty, and after descending a few floors a large elderly man joined me inside. At first he didn't seem to see me because I was standing in the corner. When the doors closed shut and he turned to look around, a strange thing happened. He took one look at me and his eyes became wide. He started turning red and breathing very heavily while pushing himself against the wall as far away from me as possible. He continued to breathe heavily and watched me in horror as I stood there. I have no idea what he was thinking, just that he was genuinely horrified of me. I felt like telling the man that I was just an ordinary person going home after a long day at work, but I was afraid to do anything because from the looks of it the only thing he really had left to do was start pounding on the door yelling, "Help! Let me out!"

The armored truck

One day in spring, I went to the Famous Players theatre to book advance tickets to the movie *Spiderman* for my brother's birthday. As I parked my car I noticed that an armoured police car drove up to the entrance of the theatre and with it came an unmarked police car with an officer inside. As I got out of my car and started walking towards the door, I felt as if I was being followed, and I tilted my head just a little so that it was not obvious that I was trying to look behind me. To my surprise, I saw the unmarked car following me the entire time as I walked down the sidewalk and up the path into the theatre. I don't know what they were thinking about me, but I definitely felt scared. If police officers are suspecting us hijabi's for terrorist crimes, then what happens in the event of a real incident where a woman wearing the hijab is involved in some kind of trouble? It makes you wonder whether the officer would believe you or the other person. When I exited the theatre, the unmarked car was waiting outside. It followed me down the path, out the parking lot and onto the main street.

The department store

Recently, I walked into a department store to buy my favourite fragrance: Pure Poison by Christian Dior. It's got a flowery smell with a hint of musk in it, which I really like. So off I went to the fragrance counter to ask the lady for Pure Poison. When I asked her for the fragrance, she looked at me in shock and maybe even disgust. At first I didn't understand the reaction,

I was confused; but then when I thought about it I realized what had happened. The idea of me, a visible Muslim woman, asking for Pure Poison was a shock to her. I eventually did get across that it was a fragrance by Christian Dior and she found the bottle. Given the level of ignorance that I had experienced, I didn't purchase the bottle on a matter of principle, nor have I gone back to that department store again.

The coffee shop

One day when my friends and I were travelling back from the United States, we stopped off at a coffee shop. My friends and I were all visibly Muslim girls having fun talking as we drank our coffee. It was interesting to see the expression on the faces of the mainly white Caucasian people that came into the coffee shop. They looked at us and seemed a bit perturbed and even a bit concerned as they walked by us. We couldn't understand what would make them feel that way, considering we were just being ourselves, until we noticed the sign next to us that said: "If you see something, say something! Call the Anti-Terrorist Hotline today!"

In addition to these somewhat ignorant or humorous events, I also went through a far more serious and traumatic experience.

The knitting lesson gone wrong

This distressing experience happened one day when I was on my way to my auntie's house for my first knitting lesson—a new-found interest that I had recently acquired. I had bought my knitting needles and had spent hours looking for the perfect colour combination for my first knitted sweater. I parked my car, walked into the lobby and got into her apartment building elevator.

As I walked into the lobby, I was followed in by a man in a white and yellow striped shirt and white shorts. He had this strange look about him. When we got into the elevator he came and stood very close to me and he became progressively closer as the elevator continued up through the floors. When the doors opened, I turn around and told him to back off, but his next comment made me realize that I was clearly being a victim of Islamophobia. He said, "Oh you Muslims are being bad, I'll show you what it means to be bad, you Muslim!" Then he attacked me in the middle of an apartment building corridor on the 4th floor.

When he first tried to put his hands on me I was completely stunned. I couldn't even understand how someone would even think to touch me. Thoughts raced through my mind like: What's going on? How is this even possible? This isn't happening! It can't be! He held me down by my shoulders and tried to rip my hijab. Then before he could tear my abaya and sexually assault me, I came to my senses and realized that the only way to get out of this was for me to take control of the situation. Somehow by the grace of Allah* I got the adrenaline rush I needed to push him off, run and knock on the first apartment door I came to. He was quick to run off.

Genderization of Islamophobia

Some say that because the attempted attack was of a sexual nature, it does not fit under the umbrella of Islamophobia. I beg to differ on this point. A close friend of mine helped me do some research and together we came to the conclusion that what I experienced was the "genderization" of Islamophobia. Genderization is really the different treatment of women versus men in the context of hate crimes. As a woman, hate often comes in the form of rape or assault; while for a man, he is often physically harmed by other men as opposed to being sexually attacked.

I collected myself quickly, picked up my bag of yarn and walked towards my auntie's door. I knocked and she opened the door. To this day, I don't know how much they heard or what they were thinking, but both auntie and my cousin Ameen were very concerned. Auntie made sure that Ameen, who was a little younger than me, walked me down the corridor, down the elevator and back to my car. He waited until I got in and drove away, making sure I was safely on my way home. When I got home, I told my mom and asked her what I should do. She was very scared and told me to keep it to myself. Growing up in this society, I was always told that any injustice should be reported and rights should always be fought for, but in my parent's case it was their belief that injustice occurs. They thought that by bringing it to the forefront would just make it even worse, and the stigma and community shame would hurt me even more emotionally. As parents, they felt that silence was the key to this whole situation.

Chastity versus justice. Faith versus safety

As South Asians and Muslims we are taught that our *izzat* (chastity), in the case of women, is the most important thing she can have. It's basically the credibility or reputation that a woman must maintain—she must be a virgin before marriage. If for some reason this reputation is broken, intentionally or unintentionally, a woman is considered "impure" and shunned from the family. As a result, any act or incident a woman may have experienced related to abuse and assault is swept under the rug for fear of losing the family's honour. In many cases, this also means that women endure much more and are prevented from discussing and receiving the proper treatment simply out of fear that others in the community may learn about the incident. This could affect not just her, but also extends to opportunities her siblings may have for marriage in the future.

Because of the nature of our community, I was asked to refrain from sharing this experience with anyone. This really had a toll on my health and my psychological well-being. I lost all self-confidence and my self-esteem went very low. I also became unable to express loving physical contact with even my closest family and friends. Let's just say, that is the single most important reason that pushed me onto the path to start my journey.

Seeing me in this state, my father was convinced that the only way to prevent such incidences in the future was for me to remove my hijab and not identify myself as a Muslim. To me, this was an impossible request which under no circumstances would I concede to. I understood where my father was coming from, but in my mind, it was like saying, "Allah* I trust you, but just to be safe I'm going to deny your message temporarily."

After the incident I completely withdrew from my family. The girl that once lit the house with her presence had suddenly gone quiet; no one knew when I came or went. I began living in a silo by myself with little interaction with anyone else. I felt anger, hatred and frustration with myself for not being able to protect myself. I was confused, and couldn't understand what I had done to make that man come towards me even though I was covered from head-to-toe. I mean really—why would someone approach someone like me? I was wearing a full black abaya, a black scarf, black shoes and black gloves.

I began dressing with multiple layers just so I could hide myself from others that may try to do a similar thing. At the same time, I made a point of not wearing the abaya anymore, even though I had made that personal choice earlier in my life to wear it for as long as I lived. There was a time when my abaya was something I considered as a safeguard for myself. I would never leave home without it. Even when my father had newcomer relatives over that stayed longer than a month at a time, I still made a point of wearing it at home. Since I stopped wearing the abaya, I also started applying increased amounts of makeup, thinking that this was the only way I was presentable enough to be in front of others.

Granted, I could have been wearing just the hijab and perhaps the same thing would have still happened, but in my mind it was something that maybe could have been prevented had I not worn the abaya. I guess in some ways I could now relate to how all those Muslim women felt who chose to take off their hijabs after 9/11.

Denial or betrayal?

My mother was very concerned for my well-being, seeing that I had almost stopped eating and speaking completely. I was in a place where I had no idea what was happening or what I was doing. Frankly, at that point I didn't really care either. The topic was kept quiet at home. I used to have nightmares all of the time. Dreams of running from people, being left alone and having no one to turn to, or being left alone in the middle of the ocean with a shark in front of me. My family didn't feel comfortable, like many, to discuss these issues with me. They were there for me, but were unable to relate to me emotionally. So in a way I also felt a betrayal from my family for not stepping up to the plate and informing the authorities out of fear that somehow the community would find out. Parents from India don't know how to deal with such issues, but not knowing how to deal with an issue doesn't mean you sweep it under the rug. At the end of the day, it's the issue of non-disclosure that really hurt. I'm writing this not to point fingers at my parents, but rather to make a point. As South Asians we're socialized to keep such issues bottled up inside. We need to have a paradigm shift on how we see such issues, and really take time to reflect on the impact it has on people.

Losing the vision

Given this situation and the stress I was experiencing, I withdrew from everything. I felt as though happiness had left my life and my world forever. I still went to work, but apart from that I did my best to stay home alone in my room just trying to keep myself busy so I wouldn't have to remember the flashes that kept coming into my mind every few minutes. I lost all notion of pursuing my dreams. I mean what was the point? My dreams of being the vice president of a financial institution, or completing my MBA and buying my ideal house suddenly didn't feel achievable. How could they be when I didn't have the confidence to even speak to people. Worse, how could I pursue my dreams when there was absolutely no support from my family. My work colleagues noticed the difference in me, but they thought it was simply because I was dealing with so many ignorant people after 9/11. Never once did they realize that it was something else that I had experienced; and never did I mention it to them. It was a long and slow process, but slowly, slowly I started regaining my self-confidence and some self-worth.

I joined the Weight Watchers at Work program hoping that this would help me relax, lose some weight and increase my self-confidence a little. This was what I thought was the first step to starting over.

I was a bit hesitant to go to the first session of Weight Watchers, but once I started going I began to enjoy my weekly meeting with the group of ladies. We talked about different foods and ways to prepare food to help us lose weight. It was interesting to hear people's ideas, and learning that creativity is often the key to weight loss. As long as you can find an alternative that tastes just as good as something you love, then you can learn to live without it. I've always had quite the sweet tooth, probably not as bad as my sister Afreen who lives off chocolate, but still. I guess it was a way to get the energy boost I needed to get through the day since my nights were spent with nightmares.

Soy is the answer

One of the first things I was introduced to was soy-based products at the time when soy was all the hype. Soy products were high in protein, filling, and low in fat. What more could you ask for? I went off to buy some soy-based products all excited and eager to get started with this new diet. I opened the soy pudding and dipped the spoon into it. Little did I realize that soy would be the one thing that would change my world forever. I licked the spoon and immediately felt my lips, throat, tongue and cheeks swell up beyond belief. My air passages started to tighten and I suddenly couldn't breathe. My mom was terrified when she saw how quickly my face turned red. I tried to keep my cool and ran to the medicine cabinet in the kitchen. I took two Benadryls and then sat down. After an hour or so the swelling started to go down and my face returned to normal.

Thereafter, avoiding soy products was anything but simple as so many manufactured foods contain either soy flour, soy oil or soy lecithin (to name a few of the twenty or more by-products derived from soy). As a result, even the smallest amount of soy in a product had an adverse effect on me; but it was about to get worse. Almost a year after my first allergic reaction to soy pudding, I had developed such severe allergic hypersensitivity to certain foods that my body experienced near-fatal anaphylactic shock, and I nearly died.

I remember one night having a craving for French fries, so I decided to make my own homemade wedges. In my house we have a frying pan that's filled with oil for all our deep-frying, so I cooked the wedges in the oil after my mom had fried some fish sticks for my younger siblings.

Everything was fine, but then all of a sudden I started coughing. I couldn't breathe, and this time I started shivering and vomiting, and my face, throat and mouth were visibly swollen. This went on for almost fifteen minutes, and still there was no sign of improvement. My mom decided to rush me to the hospital, and it took almost twenty-five minutes to get there in the extreme freezing rain. My mom despises driving in the rain, let alone freezing rain, but she did it (thanks Mummy, you're awesome).

When we got to the hospital, the nurse didn't understand what the problem was, and since I didn't' know why and what I was reacting to, she asked me to sit in the waiting room until the doctor was free. Three hours later, I was still in the same condition running back and forth from the washroom to the waiting room. I was so drained that I doubted I would recover. I was crying and my mom was getting more and more frustrated with the whole idea of having to sit and wait. When she went to talk to the nurse, the response she got back was: "I checked her breathing. She's bad but won't die. Please take a seat until it's your turn." Finally at 2:30 a.m. the nurse called me in and checked my breathing and my pulse. I was still bad but not as bad as it had been when I first arrived at the emergency ward. She told me that I would have to wait another hour or so before the doctor would see me, so I was to just sit on the bed and wait. I asked the nurse if she could hook me onto some oxygen, but she said that I would have to wait until the doctor felt it was okay to do so.

At this point, I became really frustrated and I walked out of the hospital with my mother. She was concerned that I should stick around, but I decided that if they were going to waste so much of my time then it must not have been as severe in their eyes as I thought it was. I got my mom to drive me home and I took two Benadryl tablets, had a few puffs of my inhaler and went to sleep. Sleeping wasn't easy as I was still having the fever and chill symptoms from before, and I was wheezing like a wild animal, but still I prayed and went to sleep hoping for a miracle.

In the morning, I felt sick to my stomach and had a bad headache, kind of like a hangover I guess, but then I wouldn't really know what that's like because I have never drank alcohol. Anyway, I wanted to find out what I had reacted to. So I made a list of what I had eaten, and it turned out that the reaction occurred from the small particles of soy that were left in the oil from the fish sticks.

After an anaphylactic reaction some of the symptoms may linger for a few days. From personal experience this includes feeling lethargic and weak, a slight swelling of cheeks and throat, and a feeling of impending doom. You feel that you are all alone and that no one can understand what you're going through. It's important to know that not only are you emotionally sensitive, but also physically sensitive too. In some cases the body enters a phase known as "reject mode," where the immune system sky-rockets and tries to protect the body from any other foods that may seem similar to the ingested food allergen.

Results of keeping it all bottled inside

Keeping everything bottled inside definitely proved to be a mistake. Little did I know that the stress from the backlash, my job and the shock from some of the Islamophobic experiences I endured, would affect my life for many years to come.

The lack of treatment from the first encounter, coupled with the emotional stress I was enduring, resulted in bodily trauma—or what some physicians would call "rejection mode." Basically, anything my body deemed to be new or different was considered a foreign substance and rejected. Food allergies result when your immune system sky-rockets in order to protect you from any foreign substances. This is widely understood to happen when your body goes through some sort of trauma.

It started with soy and then continued to anything related, and then anything cross-reactive as well. Another aspect of my food allergies was the development of airborne reactions. Airborne allergies are more common now than before, and for some people even the smell of peanuts or the smell of latex will cause an anaphylactic reaction. For me, any smell could cause a reaction, which made it exceptionally difficult to go into public spaces, including schools, workplaces, malls and subways.

In a case like this where the reaction is caused by

an apple or a peanut, you really need to be careful because you don't know how you will feel after a few minutes, hours or days. For example, you could walk into a mall and pass the food court and there's an ice cream shop serving sweets with peanuts. Maybe you walk into your own home when someone is putting together a peanut butter sandwich; and so it's better to abstain from going to places where even the tiniest amount of these foods may be present—but this is easier said than done.

In some cases, you need to prepare yourself for the worst while you try to live your life "normally." Being at home was tough for my family, and because of all of my airborne allergies they were really limited on what they could bring home. I did my best to come home late everyday. I tried leaving early (which was tough considering I was extremely medicated and feeling lethargic) and staying at work late. I took long drives because travelling through public transportation with airborne allergies was too big a risk. I went to the closest lakeshore park and watched the sunset. I felt totally alone, like I had lost a close friend or the love of my life.

George Bernard Shaw said there is no love more sincere than the love of food, and I completely agree with him. We don't realize how much we take food for granted until we actually have to live without it. In my case, the foods I had to avoid were far greater than the list of foods I could consume and smell. On the weekends I'd try to drive around to various stores like Canadian Tire, Fabricland, and any other place where I could walk around without having to worry about food smells. I frequently stopped at Chapters or Indigo bookstores in the area, and sat there for awhile away from Starbucks. I did my research on food allergies and alternative recipes. At this point in my life I was living in a state of constant fear.

From passion to panic

I have always been a music lover, and growing up I listened to everything from Dance, Rock—all the way to light Country. I also enjoyed a lot of Hip Hop and Rap, especially during high school. Because of the fear that became such a large part of my daily existence, I actually cut out all forms of Rap, Hip Hop and anything else that would remind me of the man who attacked me. This was really sad, considering that I grew up with it and loved it so much. My siblings weren't allowed to play it in the car or at home when I was around. I felt as though it was a trigger which I had the power to avoid. To fill in this void, I reverted to South Asian music, like the Bollywood stuff, which I wasn't as fond of before that point in time.

Coming close to people became a new challenge as well. By coming close, I don't mean being intimate with people, just the normal hugging, kissing and cheek pulling from parents and family that was once normal, but now became foreign and a cause of anxiety for me. An example of this is the fact that even my mom hugging me became an issue. I still remember seeing the hesitation on my mom's face when she came to wish me a happy birthday, not really sure how I would feel about it. The problem was that the sense of touch from another person immediately reminded me of something else; and for obvious reasons, I also developed a fear of men. I know that sounds funny to some people, but it's true. I had a really hard time looking and speaking to men for a while.

There was also a strong sense of fear of not knowing how to defend myself. I took self-defence classes hoping that this would help compensate for the frustration I was experiencing of not having done more to get back at "him," and for what he subjected me to due to his own insecurity and powerlessness.

This fear not only led to anger and frustration, but ultimately to self-hatred. The feeling of helplessness and insecurity also led to a lack of self-confidence and self-esteem. A lack of self-worth developed to the extent that I tried to be invisible by covering myself up with numerous layers and lots of makeup. I hoped that in some way the layers would pile on and hide the fears and the secrets that I was forced to keep inside. In addition, for the longest time I did what I could to avoid going into buildings, especially residential apartment buildings. Just the thought of going to an apartment made my stomach tense and brought on my anxiety.

I still remember the first time I went into a residential building; it was almost three years after the attack and I was dreading the experience. I ran down the corridor constantly looking behind me with the thought that someone would suddenly pop out of nowhere and start following or chasing me.

Dealing with my allergies

Growing up, I always had a discomfort to fruits, such as apples, peaches, pears, plums and grapes; but it was just to the extent of an itchy throat and watery eyes. When I experienced anaphylaxis for the first time, I had to go in for a full allergy prick test. When I got to the allergist's office I had the usual prick test on my arm, but after seeing the extreme swelling that appeared as a reaction to almost all of the foods tested, I was sent to an immunologist.

The immunologist ran the test again, but instead of performing the prick test on my arm, to my surprise, she asked to take the test on my back. When it was over, I was asked to go to a hospital to run more tests. I spent an entire day doing breathing and multiple allergy-related tests. When I finally returned to her office, she said she had good news for me. I didn't have a disease in my immune system, it was simply severe allergies. Like I didn't know that already! I mean, honestly, after all of those tests I thought she was going to prescribe me a pill and offer me a cure.

Next, I was referred to an allergy consultant. This guy was good. It turned out he had travelled the world doing research and searching for cures to food allergies. Almost eight months into my allergy journey, and after numerous tests, I finally met one person who actually had some sort of a cure ready for me. This is where I was introduced to the idea that food allergies are related to pollen. The only way to reduce my food allergies was to build resistance to pollen. That sounded simple enough, right? The only catch was that it was a long-term process that could take anywhere from one to four years, or more. At this point, I was ready to try anything.

Journal entry:

I went to the doctor's today and he asked me to undergo a full-blown allergy prick test on my hand. I reacted to a whole bunch of environment allergens, but there was one that swelled so much that it practically covered the front of my arm, and then the itchy feeling shot through my arm, up through my shoulder and into my back within a few minutes of him putting the tiny drop of it on my hand.

The doctor was surprised at what happened, and said it was ragweed. The other big ones were grass and trees. But what does that have to do with my food allergies? I don't know, although he says that they seem to be connected. He said that he didn't try food because he was concerned that if I reacted so severely to soy before, it may be even more severe and now even life threatening. So he said I should have a blood test done.

I know my dad is having a hard time coping with the whole idea of me having food allergies because he thinks that I'm just being too sensitive. He thinks that if I was tough I would learn to control my body on my own. It's too bad he doesn't understand what I'm going through. My mom is good that way; at least she's trying to understand. Although I don't think anyone can really truly understand how I'm feeling until (Allah* forbid) they were in my shoes. Well it's been a couple of weeks since my last entry and since then I've become allergic to all legumes (beans and lentils). I've always been allergic to peanuts and most North American fruits, but I was still surprised to learn that peanuts are actually beans not nuts. North American fruits contain the same pollen that trees and other plants do, which is why I'm allergic to these fruits. Beans include coffee, vanilla, lentils, green beans, peas, peanuts and more.

This is the list of things that my first diagnosis informed me I could no longer eat: legumes, soy, beans (garbanzo, kidney, lima, green and yellow string beans, green peas, citrus fruits (oranges, lemons and limes), tree fruits (apples, peaches, pears, plums, grapes, berries), nuts, honey, coconut, grains, wheat, corn and rice.

At the end of the day, I was dealing with oral allergy syndrome and cross-reactivity; meaning if I'm allergic to one allergen, then it's likely I will be allergic to others as well. This is because the immune system mistakenly reacts to a food that is similar to primary allergic food allergens. For example, if an individual is allergic to cow's milk, then they may also react to goat's milk as well.

When I entered reject mode after having anaphylaxis to soy, my body started rejecting everything I ate. It began with legumes and lentils, and then moved on to other beans. From personal experience, it seems that more and more allergies develop when you eat the same things over and over again. Unfortunately, not everyone is aware of this at the time of the occurrence; like in my case. I come from a South Asian background and meals are based on wheat and rice.

I eventually got to a point in my life where I was only able to eat vegetables and meats (excluding fish and shellfish). Being in this situation really started to make me wonder if it was really worth dealing with all of this. What was the reasoning for this? Why me? Would I ever be normal again?

CHAPTER 4

※

Hitting Rock Bottom

LESSON: When all else fails, don't give up!

*"Don't lose hope. When it gets darkest
the stars come out."*

UNKNOWN

Key Points

- How to renew your belief when all else fails
- The entrance of temporary angels in your life
- How to find that ray of light when you're standing in the dark

After my first reaction to the soy pudding, I wasn't supposed to eat anything purely soy-based. But I took it upon on myself to go back to my normal diet, never once thinking about being careful. I thought to myself, Maybe it was a fluke? A one-time exception to the rule? I had nothing to worry about, right?

Wrong!!!!

Denying my soy reaction was probably the worst mistake I ever made. It really increased the severity of the reactions to follow, to a point where it became anaphylactic or life-threatening. The more you consume something that you're allergic to, the more severe your reaction becomes. Soy seems to be in almost everything, and many derivatives of soy are used in packaged and fast foods. I had to start cooking solely at home, which ruled out working lunch meetings at my office. My allergies were now affecting my job and my livelihood.

It was clear that I had to stop consumption of products containing traces of soy until further notice. At first, I felt that further notice would just mean temporarily for a few weeks until my body got accustomed to eating it again. But I was wrong. When I clarified this with my doctor, he said it could take three to four years, or perhaps even longer. In some cases, people had to live with the threat of anaphylaxis for the rest of their lives! How was this possible? How could I continue living like this for the rest of my life? Was I prepared to stop eating out forever? Was I prepared to keep losing weight as fast as I was? Was I ready to deal with the constant comments from family and friends? Was I ready for the stares from people when they saw how difficult my breathing became when I tried eating normally at special occasions?

An apple a day keeps the doctor away

I could no longer eat the food I loved. The one loss that still angers me is the loss of apples. It was once my favourite fruit. A Red Delicious was the one thing I would give anything to have. Today, I can't even tolerate the smell of apples.

To give you an idea of what I was dealing with at the time, here's an example of my meal plan:

- Breakfast was 1 slice of pure hard-as-rock rye bread, 1 spoon of olive oil margarine with 1 glass of lactaid milk (which I was barely able to keep down).
- Lunch was 1 cup of salad (lettuce and tomatoes only) with homemade dressing (vinegar and oil only), 1 can of stuffed olives and 1 ½ cups of grape tomatoes.
- Snack would be 1 can of tropical fruit (papaya, guava and mango only).

- Dinner would be 1 cup of roasted potatoes, 1 cup of eggplant with ketchup and hot sauce, and 2 pieces of chicken or occasionally 1 can of tuna (if I was feeling well enough to keep it down).

This was my daily routine for more than six months … Sad, eh? Almost unbelievable, but it's the truth. God only knows how I mustered the patience and self-discipline needed to deal with that for months. My food allergies continued for quite some time, and as a result a few things happened.

Extreme weight loss

The only immediate positive effect of my food allergies was the extreme weight loss that came with it. Within the first month I went down 40 lb, and within the next six months I lost another 60 lb. By the end of year two I was down 120 lb, and as wonderful as it was to lose so much weight so quickly and start dropping pant sizes, it took quite a toll on my body. For someone who could not consume any natural vitamins in food, it was definitely a struggle to keep up with the needs of my body and my mind.

Patience and self-restraint

A verse from the Qur'an I often recite is: "Put your trust in Allah, and Allah is All-sufficient (as a disposer of affairs.)" (Al-Ahzab 33:3)

Imagine eating an amazing meal and your mouth turns dry. You start coughing and need something to drink. You see the drink, but the bottle won't open. This is a very small example of the type of self-restraint allergy sufferers feel when they can see, touch and smell food but they cannot consume it. When it comes to food allergies, denial can be very painful. Our physical well-being is at stake. For example, if I am allergic to apples and I decided to taste some apple sauce—I am putting my life at risk. Our feelings or cravings can sometimes push us to deny the reaction that exists. Having a gluten allergy, there were times when I used to dream about eating a doughnut, even though I knew that the reaction would be anaphylactic or live-threatening. In my case, my allergies were airborne, so not only was I dealing with the abstinence of eating foods, I also had to seclude myself to a place where the smell of these foods could not enter my body.

Self-restraint and patience are the most difficult challenges to have to deal with. It's especially difficult when what you're trying to resist is so close to you and so easy to get. Knowing that something as harmless as food—a necessity for living—can be harmful to our own well-being is hard to accept. There are times when I was tempted for long periods of time, but it's in moments like these that you need to put your faith and trust in God and hope that things will be alright.

> *"Let nothing disturb thee; let nothing dismay thee; all things pass; God never changes. Patience attains all that it strives for. He who has God finds he lacks nothing: God alone suffices."* St. Teresa of Avila (Spanish Nun, Mystic and Writer, 1515–1582)

Honestly, don't do what I did, which was to be in complete denial and continue to eat the food I was craving while all the while increasing the severity of the reaction each time it occurs. In some ways, I know I am to blame for bringing myself to a point where I became anaphylactic to soy. Had I been more careful and a little more patient, my reactions would not have gotten to that point and I probably wouldn't have experienced anaphylaxis for the first time—which actually caused me to enter into a rejection mode.

Avoiding your favourite food can be quite difficult, as I have learnt, but sometimes it's just a matter of choice regardless of how intense the cravings get. Try asking yourself if it's worth it? Will the pain you suffer after eating it be worth it? Do you want to continue making it worse, or would you rather wait it out and then eat plenty of it rather than just a little bit? I keep using the example of food because to me that was the reality of what I was dealing with; but in your case, it may be something completely different.

Losing faith

When dealing with physical and emotional issues, you begin to question your dreams, aspirations and goals; and ultimately your life's purpose. I always dreamt of living a life as an executive in a large Fortune 500 company and retiring in a large home, spending time with family and friends while living life in financial comfort. I dreamt of doing my part to help my family, and of being a sense of pride for my folks after completing my MBA. Life had a different plan for me. All my aspirations were shattered one by one. I couldn't get into university as I had planned. Coming to terms with that led me to begin my career in the workforce. At first, life was going the best it could be. Being twenty-one and having a 35K salary in a large corporation was definitely a good start. But it didn't last for long. With September 11, 2001 came discrimination and a sense of fear that I had never felt before. And finally the episode in the apartment caused a number of physical and emotional reactions that shattered the last of the aspirations that I held so dear to me. When dreams shatter, the first and most obvious response is shock, denial, and the process of questioning the decisions being made by destiny and God Almighty.

I thought about all of these things and about how I would live my life in the next few years, and possibly in the far future. I began to think that I was on my own, and became really frustrated with my life, myself and God. I couldn't understand why I was being punished for something when I had never intentionally done anything wrong. So I stopped praying, going to the mosque and reading the Qur'an. To me, there was nothing left for me to say or ask Him considering that He was the one who had put me into this predicament. My parents were very disappointed in my behaviour. They tried their best to keep me motivated and keep the faith and practice when and where I could—but to no avail. I had already isolated myself from my family, my friends and now from God. I knew I was walking into a dark alley with a very dim candle which was just about to go out, but I still went ahead, hoping for the best, on my own. I was sure that after going through all of this I could handle anything.

Even finding a confidant who will listen can make a huge difference, especially when you're trying to emerge from the depths of despair. Despair is a very

scary state to be in. As strong as one can be, it's tribulations that show us just how weak we really are
when it comes to putting our trust in Allah*.

Falling further down

Once you analyze your dreams, goals and ambitions, and you realize that they aren't going to plan,
you start to fall in your own eyes... and that's when
you realize that you have no leg to stand on. It's like
you're flying in the air and you realize that there isn't
a ground to land on. Eventually you'll keep falling
until you crash, right? Right. And that's what you call
hitting rock bottom.

I never thought I would hit rock bottom. We all
hear stories about people who lost everything and
had to struggle their entire lives in order to regain
what they lost. In my case, I can't say that I've gained
everything I lost, but I will say that regardless of
where I am today, I am grateful for everything I have
no matter how big or small. In some ways, I have
gained far more than I lost. I guess it depends on how
you look at it.

George Eliot once said that "There is no despair so
absolute as that which comes with the first moments
of our first great sorrow, when we have not yet
known what it is to have suffered and be healed, to
have despaired and have recovered hope."

Despair is when you lose all hope of living, hope of an improved situation, and you lose all faith in Allah*. This is a terrible place to be in, but certainly one that is part of human nature and one that people can easily fall into. Despair is "haram" or forbidden in Islam. It is said that if you believe Allah* is with you, then He is with you. But if you do not believe that Allah* is with you, then you're not with Him.

Despair can only go on for so long, and after a certain point one of two things will happen. Either you hurt yourself and end up in eternal despair, or you repent and ask for forgiveness and assistance. These were probably the most dark and depressing days of my life. I felt that living on my own without anyone's interference would make things better, but the reality of the world is that without Allah* and a higher being in your life, you have no spiritual connection or outlet to help you through your troubles. The challenges of this world are far too large and difficult to handle on our own. We need the help of Allah* and His many ways to reach us in order to pull us through.

After a few months in this state of despair, I broke down one night and the tears just began to flow. As a Muslim, committing suicide is something that is never forgiven no matter what the reason. It was then when I prayed sincerely to Allah* that I realized I was hopeless and helpless without His help. I begged Him to help me out of this situation that He had brought me into for whatever reason that was outside of my understanding and control. I prayed for Him to send me an angel, a friend, someone who I could speak to, someone who would listen to me and help me get through this.

CHAPTER 5

Renewal of Faith

LESSON: Renewing your faith and hope in the future

"Take the first step in faith. You don't have to see the whole staircase, just take the first step."

MARTIN LUTHER KING, JR.

Key Points

- Regaining the power to make it work
- Putting the pieces back together with what's left
- Coming to terms with what you have

"Life is supposed to be a series of peaks and valleys. The secret is to keep the valleys from becoming Grand Canyons." BERN WILLIAMS

When dealing with despair, it's important to understand what trials and tribulations are all about. Sometimes we only consider what we're feeling and not what's happening or why. I'm not saying that everything that happens is justifiable, but I am saying that whether we believe it or not, at some point, there's a reason we're being tested. And if we can somehow figure out what that reason is, then often that is the key to finding the solution.

Tribulations are essentially stressful and distressful experiences which test our patience, our endurance, and our faith. It may be asked, How can we know that Allah* is with us? My answer is that there are signs which bear testimony to it. The Prophet Muhammad† says that when Allah* loves his servant, He sends tribulations, and when He loves him most He severs their connection from everything. A great lecture that I listened to over and over during this time was Shaikh Hamza Yusuf Hanson's CD recording on the *17 Benefits of Tribulations*.

Life is scripted. Destiny is real!

Life is predestined. It's only when we put our faith in Allah* that we realize that this is the case. We also start to see how quickly things start falling into place. It is said that help will come from where you least expect it; how true. It's interesting how different people gauge what life is and the idea of destiny and coincidence. Deepak Chopra's coverage of this in his book *The Spontaneous Fulfillment of Desire* really resonated with me.

This is probably the most difficult lesson I learned through my journey—understanding that life is not in our control. To an extent life is pre-written. We can work towards our goals, but if it's not meant to be, it will never be that way. Similarly, if you're meant to go through certain experiences and learn from them, that's exactly what's going to happen.

So don't despair, put your faith in Allah*. He is the Lord of the worlds and has more power than we can imagine. If we ask Him for help, He will go out of his way to help us. They say He tests those who are dear to him. The late American football player and evangelical Christian minister Reggie White once said: "God places the heaviest burden on those who can carry its weight."

Even though the journey out of despair can seem

impossible, it's not unachievable. Take it one step at a time.

Putting life in his hands during tribulation

*"Whatever the struggle, continue the climb. It may be only one **step** to the summit."* DIANE WESTLAKE

Meeting people who have experienced tribulation is often difficult. Not everyone is willing to share their trials or tribulations with others. It's often hidden. In my case, according to Shaykh Hamza Yusuf Hanson, a renowned scholar within North America, "When you are grateful for a benefit you have received, share the blessing with others." This book is written to share the blessings that Allah* gave me in order to inspire others to have faith in Him during tribulations. Thank you Shaykh Hamza for your wisdom and kind words.

After lots of inner struggles and battles, I decided to take the step to believe that life can be normal once again. This is something that many never muster the courage to do—acknowledging that the Creator is the one who gives us tests and He's the only one who can help us out of them as well.

I know it's very difficult and we often think that we are strong enough to care for ourselves, especially when we're angry at something that we are experiencing. Turning to Allah* for help can definitely be a challenge. I remember hearing Shaykh Hamza Yusuf Hanson speak once about Allah* and the feeling of despair and anger that we as human beings feel when dealing with tribulation. His words totally blew me away:

> *"Allah is almighty; so large we can't even begin to imagine His full being. There are so many people in the world. Of the millions of creations and beings that Allah created, isn't it arrogant of us to think that Allah would go out of His way to punish us? There are many others in the world who are doing worse things than you, so why would He punish you?"*

It is said that Allah* will never burden His servants with more than they can bear, and if we walk towards Him, Allah* will run towards us and help us. Once you decide to put faith into Him and go with the flow on whatever comes your way, you realize that there is still hope left in your life. You feel as though it's less about you and more about Him. Even though on the surface you may feel like you're treading water, somewhere deep down inside you think to yourself: Considering God is all powerful, at some point a miracle can happen and things can change for the better. So keep a positive attitude and an open mind.

It may seem difficult to keep life in perspective, but trust me, by the end of this book you'll see that it all works out in the end. I guess essentially what I'm saying is that you have to love, trust and put your faith in Him to move to the next step in your journey.

Inshallah: God Willing

> "Hope is the last thing that dies in man; and though it be exceedingly deceitful, yet it is of this good use to us that while we are travelling through life it conducts us in an easier and more pleasant way to our journey's end." FRANÇOIS DE LA ROCHEFOUCAULD

As Muslims, from a young age we are told to use the term "Inshallah" (God willing) when we speak. This term teaches us that everything happens only with the willingness of God. But these days some people don't use it as often because they feel that it's simply a term people use when trying to push something off.

When a prayer is sincere enough, it's amazing how quickly and how easily life begins to change. After the difficult task of putting my faith in Allah* and just going with whatever came to me—acknowledging that I am powerless without Him, trusting Him and finding that small ray of hope deep down inside—I began to really think about my trial and why I was going through it. Perhaps there was some reason why

I had to experience what I did, and maybe there was some benefit in it.

"Adversity introduces a man to himself."
ANONYMOUS

FOOTPRINTS IN THE SAND

One night a man had a dream.
He dreamed he was walking along the beach
with the Lord.
Scenes from his life flashed across the sky,
and he noticed two sets of footprints in the sand.
One belonging to him and the other to the Lord.
When the last scene of his life had flashed before him,
he recalled that at the lowest and saddest times of his life
there was only one set of footprints.
Dismayed, he asked, "Lord, you said that once
I decided to follow you
you'd walk with me all the way.
I don't understand why, when I needed you most
you would leave me."
The Lord replied, "My precious child.
I love you and I would never leave you.
During your times of trial and suffering
when you saw only one set of footprints...
That was when I carried you."

Visual reminders

Once you put faith in Allah* He'll give you constant reminders that He's around. There will be signs throughout your journey, like street signs giving you signals on the next step to take. Sometimes, you just have to let life run on autopilot and go with the flow. It's better to live that way than to worry about things you can't control. Trust me, I've been there and done that, and it's not worth it.

The appearance of 786

 Not everyone believes in the meaning of "786" as Bismillah, meaning: In the name of God. From childhood, we are taught that we should say this before starting any action as a form of praising Allah*. For me, this was something that kept me going, and I would see 786 at key times in my life, like just before something important was going to happen or when I was feeling extremely down. It was a constant reminder for me. This is not to say that I was looking for the number wherever I went, but I did see it on license plates, store signs and in street numbers. These were random little rays of hope planted at the right places, which would appear when I needed them the most. Other examples were trucks driving by at certain times with reminders to keep my faith: *"With your best interest in mind"; "The first step to a better tomorrow"; "Here to serve you"; "Delivering a better future."* I know it sounds tough, but in the end you'll see that your life will actually improve and you'll actually get a number of benefits from your tribulation or test.

I once heard a wise proverb: "God didn't promise days without pain, laughter without sorrow, or sun without rain; but He did promise strength for the day, comfort for the tears, and light for the way. If God brings you to it, He will bring you through it."

So began the process of renewal where I did my best to pray and ask for patience and perseverance to make it through this trial. One of my life dreams has been to visit Mecca in Saudi Arabia and perform Hajj at what Muslims call the "Centre of the Universe." Through my entire journey, it's the one thing I have wanted to do the most, but unfortunately, because of my airborne allergies it was next to impossible to travel that far, get proper food and accommodation and remain healthy enough to make the religious pilgrimage. I've even dreamt I was there standing in front of the Kabah Sharif. When I awoke, I could still feel the cold marble floor on my feet and tears streaming down my face. I pray that I get the opportunity to go soon: inshallah.

Taqwa

The first thing I did once I felt a sense of renewal was to start up a clothing business under the name of "TAQWA Sports Gear." TAQWA in Arabic means *God consciousness* or *piety*.

I decided that in addition to work, I would do what I could to spread my understanding and God consciousness to others, as well as myself of course. So I designed my own Islamic sportswear for both men and women, and I began advertising and selling the items at local businesses and events.

Taqwa was started as a creative Islamic sports-wear clothing company. We had zipper hijabs (the first of their kind) and sporty sleeves for women as well as basketball jerseys and other unique items. My sister Afreen and I had started it as a partnership. We created the logo from scratch, designed each and every piece, and put in a lot of work into getting it started—which was easy. Sustaining it was the challenge. Unfortunately, after about a year, I couldn't keep up and had to close it down.

We began selling Taqwa clothing at the first MuslimFest in Mississauga at the Living Arts Centre.

One of the first customers we had was Preacher Moss—a Muslim comedian of Jamaican origin who is going around the world sharing laughter and joy with the world under the banner of: "Allah Made me Funny." And he really is! Preacher has been a good friend and has stood by me through it all (thanks Preach... you're amazing!).

If I knew who he was at the time, I wouldn't have charged him for the t-shirt; but nevertheless I was pleased that he was one of my first customers ever for Taqwa. I always felt comfortable and enjoyed myself with Preacher. I could be myself and not have to worry about anything else; which is very easy to do when Preacher is around.

Guardian angels

"Time goes by so fast; people go in and out of your life. You must never miss the opportunity to tell these people how much they mean to you."
                                        ANONYMOUS

I met Shazad Mirza at work after I hit rock bottom and prayed for repentance to Allah*. I was at my lowest of low times. The interesting thing is that I had no idea that my prayer for a friend would come true so quickly. He reassured me that life would be okay if only I chose to hold on and walk along this new and unpaved path. He was also the first guy I befriended in a long time, and he helped me develop a positive attitude and get comfortable interacting with people once again. Having met my brother Shazad, my asthma miraculously improved. As mentioned throughout this book, all of this came from Allah* and my angels are simply a *zariyah* (a means) sent from Allah*. I'm very grateful to Allah* for sending me this angel when he did.

Journal entry:

I just came back from my follow-up appointment at the immunologist, and she said that my breathing has to improve before anything else can be done about my allergies. Apparently, when you fall into anaphylaxis you loose up to 80 percent of your breathing ability—that's considering you're at 100 percent (or perfect breathing). She also told me that I was at 60 percent and that I had to get up to or as close to 100 percent as possible so that I could withstand another attack without complete loss of breathing. So now I have a whole bunch of medications to start up on. The good thing is that I don't have any sort of immune problem; they're just allergies.

During this time, Ramadan came upon us as well. Ramadan, the month of fasting, is one of the Five Pillars of Islam. Even in this state that I was in, I decided to keep fasts. It was my way of putting faith in Allah*. It was also a way of cleansing my body and my soul; and it would also help me remember the importance of food from the perspective of someone dealing with poverty, and not just food allergies like me. Keeping the fast wasn't as difficult as breaking it would be. This would not have been too bad except that during Ramadan at work, a bunch of us decided to have a daily potluck (fast breaking) group. The difficulty was that I would have to bring my own special food from home because I couldn't eat any of the food that they would be eating.

My brother Shazad was also quite the chocoholic, and knowing that I couldn't eat chocolate at the time, he made a point of bringing me dried mangos and other sweets so I could enjoy them with him. Even today, when I eat a dried mango or bite into a sesame snap, my eyes fill up with tears. Sometimes the little things people do last a lifetime.

He came like the wind, blew my sorrows away, and then three months later he found a new path. I remember having conversations with him about finding another job. I was very hopeful that he'd find what he was looking for, and made a point of waking up each night for the next few weeks before the crack of dawn (Tahjud) to pray for him. They say that Allah* appears on the first heavens during this time of the night and anything you ask is granted. I don't know if that did it or if it was his charm and wit that helped him get the job, but he got the job and was on his way to starting a whole new career. The bottom line was that he came into my life because of God's plan. If it was not for Allah*, we would have never met; and I truly believe that.

Shazad told me that when he started working at the workplace he was trying to find himself, and when he met me he realized that he could do so much more with his life. Even with the pain I was in, I had ambitions and to him that was inspiring. It's interesting how the world works sometimes.

Take it from my personal experience, if you are in despair or know someone who is, remind them or yourself that the only way to get out of this is for you to sincerely pray and believe in Allah*, God or whatever higher being you believe in. I recently read a book called *The Secret* and the law of attraction. If you put it into the Universe that you want something, it will come to you. My mom forwarded this to me as an email. It's absolutely awesome. Thanks mom!

Prayer is one of the best free gifts we receive.
I asked God for water, He gave me an ocean.
I asked God for a flower, He gave me a garden.
I asked God for a friend, He gave me all of YOU...
If God brings you to it, He will bring you through it.

Happy moments, praise God.
Difficult moments, seek God.
Quiet moments, worship God
Painful moments, trust God.
Every moment, thank God.

CHAPTER 6

A Helping Hand

LESSON: Building a Support System

"After awhile you learn that what you really are is all the experiences and all the thoughts you've ever had and all the people who have touched your life, no matter how briefly."

ANONYMOUS

Key Points

- Developing a circle of friends
- Surrounding yourself with the right people
- Helping others, while helping yourself

Family first

"Hold a friend's hand through times of trial, let her find love through a hug and a smile; but also know when it is time to let go—for every one of us must learn to grow." ANONYMOUS

Sometimes our desires and dreams become so overbearing that we don't know how to deal with them. This is especially true when we have to put our dreams on hold until we can get through the journey and to a point where we can begin to re-establish ourselves once again. For moments like these, it's essential to surround yourself with loving people. For me, I needed to heal both physically and emotionally before I could move on with my life, and so it became even more important for me to reach out.

Family are the first in line to help when you really need it. We often have our own issues with family members and lots of family politics, but when push comes to shove, you know that they will be by your side. I learnt this when my family began to see how much my food allergies were starting to affect my day-to-day life. Not so much with the emotional issues that I was dealing with, but definitely the physical ones.

At times, it was a bit frustrating because we were all learning as we went along, and so there were moments I would get sick because a new food substance would enter our home. My family tried their best and suffered with me because a lot of foods weren't allowed in the house when I was around. I ended up spending most of my time in my room, and then later on in the basement apartment we had.

The supportive family members were always there for me, making sure that they learned as much about the problem as possible; like my mother and my siblings. They are the ones trying to go out of their way to make you happy in small ways. Like the time my six-year-old sister decided to boil strips of cabbage in water and serve it to me with tomato sauce because I had a gluten allergy and was craving spaghetti. I remember the time my mom went out of her way to get me a gluten-free cake for my birthday, even though it cost a fortune ($40 for something that fed four people!).

It's these people who make all the difference in the world, and you need people like this to help you keep going. It's also these people who you generally live with, like your immediate family who make sure that there is no cross-contamination of any kind. In my case, my allergies were so severe my mom made arrangements for me to move into the furnished basement so I had access to my own kitchen and stove. I certainly appreciated the gesture. It was better than having to sit in my room while others ate, or to go for a long drive or walk while my family ate dinner together. Keep in mind that my allergies were airborne as well.

The unsupportive family members are those who just don't understand how someone can be allergic to food. They're usually the ones like my father who said things like, "Oh, it's all in your head," or, "You're just being overly-sensitive," or even, "Take control of yourself. Eat what you want. Nothing will happen. Look at me. I'm fine and I can eat everything."

Journal entry:

When I went over to my auntie's house yesterday, I took along my own food just to be on the safe side. She was offended that I wasn't eating what she had prepared. I told her that it's not that I didn't want it; rather that I couldn't have it. It's amazing how people take so much for granted that they don't have to take the time to look at everything. My dad felt bad about how my aunt was feeling and told me to eat something.

The only thing that I could possibly eat was an Indian sweet carrot bar, but even that could have been dipped or made with some sort of oil. He said that even if they did use it, it would be some very small traces so I should be fine. After all, it's just oil right? So I decided to take the chance and went ahead and ate it. That was definitely a mistake because I started reacting immediately and had to leave her house as soon as possible. My dad was shocked because it was the first time he was actually with me at the time of a reaction. He became terrified when he started to see the instant swelling of my throat, the coughing, the wheezing and more. From that day on, he vowed to never say anything, and fully accepted the problem.

So, if you have someone like that in your family, don't be too hard on them. They may just be in a state of denial or may just be ignorant about the issue. Try to do your best to educate them about the issue. Don't be like me. Don't take the chance. It's not worth it.

Family is family, and no matter what they say they always stick it through with you. My family sacrificed a lot for me. They didn't eat many things they wanted to just because I was around. I appreciate all they did for me.

Supportive friends

God works in mysterious ways. Family and close friends are an ongoing support, but sometimes you need a temporary support system to help you move from one step to the next.

I have had amazing friends in my life, and a few very close ones like Sanjitha Ranjan who has stood by me throughout my journey. They've shared my tears, my anger, my depression; and most recently—my happiness. It's said that the best mirror is an old friend, and that's definitely the case with Sanjitha and me.

> *"We all take different paths in life, but no matter where we go, we take a little of each other everywhere."* TIM MCGRAW

Throughout my story, a number of angels or soulmates came in and out of my life at the right time. These are the people that, in addition to the ongoing support of family and close friends, were around and found me when I needed them the most. Most of these people say that they were just being themselves, and for them that's the truth; but for me, just the fact that they were there made all the difference. For that, I'm forever grateful, and I hope that I have the chance to do the same for them as well.

The net effect of a soulmate on your life will always be positive. The whole point of a soulmate turning up in your life is to show you to yourself. That is the purpose of all human relationships. You learn through viewing in the mirror. They are in your life temporarily for you to learn or for them to learn something from you, and you can have multiple soulmates in your life. It's believed that soulmates were the souls around you when you were first created, and the closest of these soulmates are placed on this earth as a family and others you meet throughout your life here and there. I don't know if this is a fact, but I certainly appreciate the thought.

When the fire alarm went off at work in the middle of winter, it was freezing. It was the last day I would see Shazad Mirza for a very long time, and the first day another angel would enter my life. A young man wearing a long trench coat came up to me and said, "Assalamu alaikum. Have you heard of Zamzam?"

Zamzam water is a holy water from Mecca that has many medicinal properties. It is said that it can make the blind see and that it is the cure for all medical ailments. Coincidence? I think not. Why hadn't I thought about this before? It was a clear sign that Zamzam was needed to help cure my ailment. The *shifa* (cure) came from Allah*, and now that I had put faith in Him, He was helping me take the next step. It turned out that this young man, Rehan Saeed, was a wholesaler of Zamzam spring water bottles. From that day on, I spent the next two years solely drinking Zamzam water with the intention that my allergies would heal. Rehan made sure I was always stocked with a supply, and so I literally drank nothing but Zamzam daily. Not only did I start to get physically better, but this was the first step in my life towards the spiritual healing as well.

Rehan taught me a lot about the importance of earning money in a halal way, and he explained to me the severity of dealing with *ribba*. He was also the first one who introduced me to the concept of Islamic banking and finance. Little did I know at the time, that many years later he would be there to help me with my student loan project. We are still in touch today, and are still working on finding a solution for this ever growing problem of interest-based student loans which are really causing students financial hardship; Muslim and non-Muslim.

After two years of providing me with Zamzam and changing my whole outlook on life, Rehan left my workplace and the country to pursue his education in Islamic finance.

A life map

My cousin Parveen had heard about my allergies and my problems and offered to take me out to dinner. It was a challenge to find a place I could eat at, considering most places were cooking with vegetable oil and served wheat. In the end I was able to find an Iranian restaurant in North York called The North. It was awesome. Since I had recently developed a resistance to rice, I was able to eat their Sultani kebab platter, which was basically rice, a roasted tomato and a grilled beef kebab marinated in pomegranate juice.

This is the same restaurant that I had my birthday party dinner six months later when I was cured of my wheat allergy.

During this time, Parveen helped me re-evaluate my life, and she gave me *The Book of Secrets* by Deepak Chopra. Reading this book changed my life forever, and I took out time to do some inner reflection. After doing my own research online too, I came up with the following: A life map. Some people may think of this as being something childish, but for me it helped to put things into perspective. There are some things that I have accomplished and others that I still need to accomplish, but it's a nice visual to have around to keep you motivated on a day-to-day basis.

The basic idea is to create a collage by taking a pile of magazines and catalogues (if you're too tidy to have old magazines sitting around then round them up from the neighbours), and start cutting out words and pictures that speak to you or evoke feelings. Once you've done that, start gluing them to a large sheet of paper. When you're finished, ask yourself:

- What have I learned about myself from looking at my life map?
- Do I see any patterns?
- Does anything on my life map surprise me?
- If I knew that all of the images on this life map

would come into my life, would I be okay with that?
- Who do I need to become in order to fulfill the intentions on my life map?
- Based on my life map, what quality will I commit to developing this year?

A life map is a great way to look inside and pull amazing jewels out of the depths of your heart and mind; and also to discover the fun things that you enjoy. Here's how mine turned out: My fascination is clouds, and I have an aspiration to see the Northern Lights. My goals included wanting to work at United Way, and in the charity sector; working and traveling; and going to hajj in Mecca. This all came out on my life map. It got me excited, and I realized for the first time after a long period why life is important. Without life, how can I aspire to achieve my dreams? The question that comes to mind is: What would you do if money didn't matter?

So go ahead and try it. You never know it may be just what you need. The sky is the limit. Go for it!

Since my life map is on my laptop, which I take to work with me, people often get a chance to see it. I put it up to remind myself of the things I want to do, and to keep myself motivated. Sometimes, I find it interests others and even inspires them to do things that they love. For example, when I was applying for my job at United Way I was asked to do a presentation. When I put up the projector, the interviewer saw my life map and asked if she could see it. She was pleased to see United Way as one of my goals. Another person in the office saw it as she was walking by my cubicle. In asking what it was, I explained it to her briefly and told her that I would bring in the book for her so she could do it herself. A few days later, before I had a chance to bring in the book, she came back to me and thanked me. I wasn't sure for what, but then she told me that just by seeing my life map she realized that one of her life goals is to learn violin, and so she joined violin classes, which she was very excited about.

CHAPTER 7

✹

A Change of Direction

LESSON: Accepting Life for what it is and making the most of it

"Life is a series of natural and spontaneous changes. Don't resist them— that only creates sorrow. Let reality be reality. Let things flow naturally forward in whatever way they like."

LAO-TZU

Key Points

- Be persistent
- Keep rolling with the punches
- There's always light at the end of the tunnel
- Be brave. Face your fears!

Dealing with workplace politics

Dr. Raymond Lindquist is the author of the book *Notes for Living,* and a former long-standing pastor at the Hollywood Presbyterian Church in Hollywood, California. He famously said that, "Courage is the power to let go of the familiar." Courage is an integral part of moving on. Without courage, you're left stuck in a place where everything stays the same, and you find yourself dwelling on the same issues over and over again. It takes a lot of time, effort and *himmat* (strength) to be courageous enough to move on, and when you have it, it's more important to you at that point than anything else in the world.

Things become much worse before they get better, and this was especially true with my allergies. At first, I was still able to function at work, especially with the support of my two angels. When I told my manager about my health issues and the need to tell the team, she understood the necessity to tell my colleagues about the triggers, symptoms, reactions and emergency procedures involved. People acted a bit strange and started to make jokes to break the ice.

People began to be cautious; some would ask questions to make sure the foods they were eating were okay, and others seemed to go about as usual. Let's just say I had a lot of reactions at work because of the unintentional food allergens in the air. I was allergic to peanuts, and this was made clear to everyone at work. Every day for a week, I came into work and the moment I walked to my desk I felt sick. My asthma would kick in, I would feel sluggish and lethargic, feverish, and swelling would occur in my mouth, throat and tongue. I tried to work but the medication made me drowsy. I really tried hanging in there, but as the days of the week went on it got worse. So finally on Friday, I decided to pull myself together and investigate the cause of my suffering. Lo and behold, it turned out that my colleague was eating peanut-butter sandwiches for breakfast half an hour before I came into work each day. He left the remains of the packaging in the garbage box next to my cubicle and didn't realize that the wrapper and part of the crust in his garbage bin would make me react so severely.

Unfortunately, as the months went on, my asthma went from bad to worse and I was falling behind on my work due to absences. Many times I'd have to leave work after someone opened an orange and stunk up the floor, or warmed something strong in the microwave. I approached the human resources department to see if there was any way of placing signs on the doors asking people to refrain from eating certain foods. I was told that this would be considered a violation of both human rights and employee rights; and so they could not ask anyone to refrain eating at their desks. I was furious. I was between a rock and a hard place because I now knew why I was getting sick, and there was nothing I could do about it. The days went on, and by the end of six months or so I received my first warning letter. My manager was getting quite frustrated at my attendance record, and I was getting annoyed that I was unable to get any better without their cooperation. There are three warning letters, and the final one is a pink slip. I told my manager that there's nothing I can really do if I keep developing allergies to new foods. It was not like I could predict what food I'll become allergic to next. Unfortunately, my manager didn't share my view, and told me that only if I could stay absent-free for the next six months would she drop the first letter from my record. Otherwise, I'd get another letter for each additional absence, starting from that day onwards.

This was definitely not a fun situation to be in, and I managed to stay at work for another few months before my second and third warning letters were issued. It was then finally time for my performance review. I'll never forget that day. It was the Friday before Canada Day and I was looking forward to the long weekend. My manager and I were on okay terms, although she seemed a bit on the edge with me in the preceding days. So when she called me in, I figured she would be a bit stern about my absences, but to my surprise something completely different occurred. She sat me down, and said, "Farheen, you've worked here for a long time and you're a good worker, but I'm sorry to say I don't want you to work here anymore." I was stunned! How could she ask me to leave just like that? I'd worked in a specialized role for the company for the last four years. How could she just ask me to go? She went on to say, "You and I both know I can't fire you, so I expect to see your resignation on Monday morning. Don't bother coming in on Monday." She left after saying that, and I was left in the room alone crying my eyes out, completely confused and unsure of what to do. I left work early that day and drove home thinking about the decision I had to make. When I got home, I spoke to my mom and dad and they both said that I should hang in there and fight for what I believe in. I knew that if I quit, I would lose my severance and any other money I could get, but deep down in my heart I knew staying would just make me even more sensitive and weak. After speaking to some more of my elder relatives and a few random lawyers on the phone, I decided to send in my resignation. Surprised? Yeah I know, I was surprised too—but there's a twist.

I emailed my resignation to my manager on Monday morning, just like she asked, but I also copied in my human resources consultant, the vice president and the CEO of the organization. Yep! If I was going to go, then everyone should know why and that my resignation was only based on my manager's request. I had been working for the company for four years, and had received the quarterly employee award twice since I began. I couldn't just leave without telling anyone about it.

At first, I thought that was it. There was total silence. I decided to stay home and spend the next few months relaxing. The first week was very quiet. I slept, ate what little I could, and spent time at home watching TV and catching up on my soaps. On the following Monday, to my surprise, I received a call from a different HR consultant asking if I would reconsider. I told her what had happened and that in order for me to come back I would need some sort of accommodation of my needs. She agreed and said I would be on paid leave until they came up with a solution. She said she'd be in touch on a biweekly basis until they were ready for me to return. I got to stay home and get paid for it. Yay! So I did. I stayed home for three months in total, and finally after a long and relaxing wait, I was called into work.

There were two surprises waiting for me when I returned. The first was finding out that my manager had been fired the day I emailed the letter to her (I recently reconnected with her on Facebook and added her as a friend. I don't blame her for what happened. I know we were both going through a learning curve at the time). The second was that they had built me a separate office off the main floor with a glass door and window. I was to stay in my own room and work there, and I was not permitted to enter the main floor working area at any time. I had my own computer, my own cabinets, and I brought in my books, my radio, and other things to help keep me occupied for eight hours a day on my own. They even provided me with my own water cooler and an air purifier to make sure that no food odours would enter in at any time. Things were getting better and I didn't feel any reactions. I was completely alone and free to work and do what I wanted to do. My sensitivity to food was finally starting to reduce because of the very few reactions that were occurring. There was still the odd reaction happening at home or outside, but luckily not at work.

For the most part, I was happy with the way things were, and so I managed to stay for two years in that small room with the little glass door. After a while, the lack of human interaction really started to get to me. I couldn't deal with just being on my own for so long each and every day; especially since, even at home, I would have to go and sit in my room or drive around so that others could eat. Essentially, I was living in a bubble for two years. After a while, my doctor said that I was starting to develop feelings similar to people held in solitary confinement, and that the only way I could continue working at my job was to take anxiety pills. I wasn't prepared to do that, but I also did not know what else to do other than to stay at work. With the health condition I was in, there was no way I could get another job, and so I tried to stay as long as I could with occasional visitors to my "glass box" from Farah, Carolyn and Philomena making it more bearable.

When I was at that point when I felt completely stuck and restricted, I met Gary Bond. Gary was hired by my workplace to come and speak to everyone about possible career growth in the company. I still remember him asking me where I wanted to go within the company. I knew I couldn't go anywhere. When I told him about my isolation at work, he took me aside and said, "Look you know moving in this company won't happen. Why don't you wait a few minutes after the session and we'll talk." So I did, and when the session was over he asked me to bring him a copy of my resume. He said he'd help me work on it and was surprised at the number of volunteer positions I had held.

Gary suggested that I consider something outside of this workplace, something in the non-profit sector. This way I could help others and get job satisfaction. In most cases I would be on the road, so I wouldn't have to deal with a lot of the food issues that exist in an office environment. I was all for it, especially since I was very involved with volunteering in the community whenever I could. He gave me some suggestions on my resume and asked me to email him a soft copy. After half a dozen emails back-and-forth he sent me the final version. It's evident to me that Gary played a key role in helping me gain the strategy and the confidence I needed to move on, but before I could move on to other opportunities, I would need to really get a handle on my physical health first.

Breaking out of solitude

I was ready to quit my job, but first I wanted to work on getting better. So, the first thing I did was go through a full course of immunotherapy. I had initially started this when it was recommended by my allergy consultant. He said that the root of all my food allergies was the fact that I was allergic to North American pollen.

Injecting small amounts into my body on a weekly basis, week-by-week for one month, is the treatment of immunotherapy. You won't see the results of the immunotherapy until at least four to six months, but you will see a difference. The process itself is very tiring as you can experience any (and all) symptoms in the form of a reaction. For most people it's just the swelling of the arm, some hay fever symptoms, and generally the feeling of being lethargic. In fact, right afterwards I felt even more sensitive and tired than before, but I just kept taking antihistamines and having faith.

Because of the severity of my reactions, this process was extremely painful. To be honest, I don't remember most of what I experienced because of how it affected me. I was injected with Pollen-x R weekly for one month during the summer just before the ragweed season. I would take Friday afternoons off work to take the shots so that I'd be well enough to go back into work on Monday mornings. The reality is that I don't remember anything between the time I took the shot on Friday afternoon until Monday morning. I vaguely remember my mother coming into my room and feeding me soup at random times during the weekend, but other than that it's all a blur. There was a point during this time that I was taking three or four Reactine 20 mg tablets (the normal dosage of Reactine over the counter extra strength is 5 mg). After going through the therapy for three years, I finally got to a place where I felt only the common symptoms after taking the shot.

Once the summer and my immunotherapy were both over, I spent my time working on small projects here and there. Now that I had limited friends at work and even fewer in my personal life, I decided to take my first step to moving on. A friend of mine, Farah Quadri, had been a close former colleague at work, and suggested that I go with her to a dinner for a

Muslim professionals' social networking group: The Council for Advancement of Muslim Professionals (CAMP).

I dressed up in a burgundy dress and went to the first dinner I had gone to in a very long time. At the dinner, I met a bunch of new friends, including Shahzad Ghaznavi and Urz Heer, who were very helpful and arranged food that I could eat. They even labelled all of the food dishes with all of the ingredients so I knew exactly what to expect, and they welcomed me with open arms. Today I am the president of this organization in the Greater Toronto Area.

Having become so used to isolation, it was hard for me to jump right into a large group of people without feeling intimidated. Two-and-a-half years of isolation can do that to you.

When I became the president of CAMP, I literally took the plunge from a single person world to a place where I was making speeches to over three hundred people at a time. There were a few dilemmas for me to deal with here. Because I had dropped 120 lb, I would have to buy a whole new wardrobe. The other part I had to really struggle with was the idea of sitting and eating with other people.

The main aim of CAMP is to help young Muslim professionals advance, and we do this by offering a variety of events—professional, social and community. The way I see it, we are the future of tomorrow, and as such it's my responsibility to make a contribution to Canadian society. I believe that as a Muslim Canadian professional, young people are the future of this beautiful country that we call our home. We must take it upon ourselves to be engaged and involved. I also strongly feel that we should embrace our identity and be proud of who we are. We can't divide values from identity. There's been a lot of damage done to our image as Muslims, and we have the opportunity to change that through our actions and our contributions to the broader community.

Halal student financing

In May 2007, CAMP hosted a panel discussion on Islamic finance. Some of the speakers that were invited included people like Rushdi Siddiqui, who is the Global Director of the Islamic Indexes at the Dow Jones. Many Muslims are often skeptical about using Islamic finance options versus conventional banking, but we all acknowledge that using *ribba* is forbidden (*haram*). There are many reasons for this—mainly that *ribba* is money that we don't actually earn, which is seen as unfair. In Islam, any money transaction must be backed against an asset, and so we can't lend money for money.

What Mr. Siddiqui said at the panel discussion resonated with me, and I kept pondering on this point. I knew there was something I could do, but I wasn't sure what. Then I realized that we have a need for affordable and accessible interest-free student loans for Muslims. Since I used to work at the Government service provider for student loans, where I was a Knowledge Analyst and had the opportunity to work on projects, I really thought the idea could work. Around the same time, I had heard about the Crescent Entrepreneurs Association, which is an organization started by a few people including Urz Heer (someone I consider to be my mentor and the door to the community, and CAMP). The objective of the Association is to inspire young people with the spirit of entrepreneurship through a business competition. I decided to enter my project into the competition.

I named the plan "ILM Financial: Interest-free Loan Management" (ILM also means "knowledge" in Arabic). That night after submitting the proposal, when I fell asleep, I dreamt about the *seal of the prophet*, which is the ring that the Prophet Muhammad[†] used to seal all of his transactions. It was definitely a good sign. I met a friend during this process, Mubashir Iqbal, who believed in the project and helped me along the way.

To prepare for the competition, I practiced hard and made sure I knew exactly what I was going to say. The night before the competition, I fell ill from exposure to apple and wasn't sure if I would make it. I did what I could to relax and stay medicated, and I focused on trying to get better. In the morning, I managed to make it to the location early. I was medicated and feeling quite groggy, but I still tried to remain as coherent as possible. My friend was already there when I arrived, and came over to see me. He asked me if I was nervous and I said "yes." He said, "Think as though you have already done the presentation and it's five minutes after the fact. This will help calm you down." Throughout the day I was exposed to many bottles of apple juice, and I knew I was going downhill but I just kept holding on, and by the grace of Allah* I managed to make it through.

I won the CEA competition and got $1,200 as a prize for the seed money to start up my idea. I thanked everyone for their help and support in my acceptance, all except Mubashir. I wanted to thank him personally, but I was so overwhelmed I left without saying thank you or goodbye. I don't know how I got home that evening. I literally cried from the moment I left the competition until the moment I got home—and it's a forty-five minute drive. The tears of joy just wouldn't stop flowing, and I was overjoyed and speechless. This was the first time in my life that I felt true gratification.

Mubashir Iqbal, another one of my angels, taught me that life is not just about getting by, it's about aspiring to achieve your dreams no matter how large, challenging or outrageous they may be. For that lesson I'm truly grateful. Meeting him really helped me plunge into the world of dreams... my dreams; ones that I had given up on so long ago (thanks Mub!). Since then, I took a dive back into the community and once again found the energy to actively participate and contribute. Let's just say I'm playing catch up!

CHAPTER 8

A New Tomorrow

LESSON: A new beginning; living and discovering its purpose

"I have one life and one chance to make it count for something... I'm free to choose what that something is, and the something I've chosen is my faith. Now, my faith goes beyond theology and religion and requires considerable work and effort. My faith demands—this is not optional—that I do whatever I can, wherever I am, whenever I can, for as long as I can with whatever I have to try to make a difference."

JIMMY CARTER

Key Points

- The importance of leaving a legacy behind
- Realizing that life's purpose is more than just personal gain

Learning to:

- Put your mind towards anything you want to achieve
- Trust God, take risks and know that he'll help you through it

Key Points (*cont'd*)

- Be persistent
- Have pure intentions
- Always be fair, kind and supportive to others
- Building a positive network is so important

Once I started to see improvements in my state of health, I decided to take my first step in living life normally once again. I kept a positive attitude and remained persistent despite a minor reaction from my reintroduction. There were times when I was fine and I could achieve a lot of work in one day, and other times when I couldn't get out of bed for days. Having the added support system of my family and friends really made a difference. Since I wanted to live life "normally again", I decided not to share my story with the new people that entered my life.

A fresh start: Doing what you enjoy and being strategic in your choices

> *"Everyone has been made for some particular work, and the desire for that work has been put in every heart."* RUMI (13TH-CENTURY PERSIAN POET)

Over the years, I have done many paid and voluntary jobs in the non-profit sector. In a way, I feel like I have been given a new lease on life, and I'm trying to play catch up in order to make up for the time in isolation. I now want to spend the rest of my life working for the betterment of others. This is my way of giving back and helping others deal with whatever trial they may be facing. I may not be able to completely empathize with everyone, but I can certainly be there to support and listen to others, as they have done for me. It's also my little effort to express my gratitude to Allah* for what he has given me. There are many ways to express gratitude, so reflect and acknowledge what you have been given and find an opportunity to give back some of it.

Even if you can't afford to give a penny to others, then give your time; and if you can't give your time, then give a smile. Time and effort (and even a smile) are also considered a form of charity or *Sadaqah* in Islam. They say that each human being influences four people each day. Imagine if you can double that or even triple it?

> "We live life with what we get, but we make a life with what we give." WINSTON CHURCHILL

The first step to getting involved in the non-profit sector is to learn about a variety of charities. There is something out there for everyone, and there are many websites and groups that you can visit. The one that I love is *charityvillage.com*.

My first such non-profit experience was working with Louise Russo and her Walk Against Violence Everywhere (WAVE) campaign. Louise's challenge was to engage youth in extra-curricular activities by way of a scholarship in an effort to end violence everywhere. Louise herself had been a victim of violence, which ultimately took away her ability to walk. Through this experience, I realized how helpless one can be and how fortunate we are to be able to walk. I also learnt how you can be compassionate with others, even in the adverse situation you are in.

After working with Louise my allergies were almost 90 percent cured. I had been given a second chance, and I decided to continue working in the non-profit sector even though I was in a position to go back and work for the commercial corporations and make the big bucks like before. Giving back through my work and efforts, now that I was healthy enough to work, was a blessing that still gives me satisfaction.

Throughout my life, I learnt that God is with me at all times, and I have tried to develop a God consciousness within. Just knowing that I was able to breathe freely each and every day became a reminder for me. I was reminded that my every breath, my every bite, and that every moment of my life was a precious gift from God.

Realizing that each and every grain of food is from God, and that the ability for me to ingest something that I was deathly allergic to the smell of before, is a remembrance each and every day of how lucky I am to be alive. Knowing that I have been given a second chance to work and help others that are in worse situations, is a reminder that had it not been for God, I could not have been where I am today.

*"Happiness is not a reward—it is a consequence.
Suffering is not a punishment—it is a result."*
LAO-TZU

I may sound crazy when I say this, but my goal in life is to end poverty in the city and beyond. My friends always tell me to do one thing at a time, but to me, everything is equally important. I guess the idea is, even if I am able to start a ripple in the water, eventually others will come along and produce the tidal wave needed to make the change. The mission statement of United Way of York Region is an inspiration to my own cause: *"To improve lives and build community by engaging individuals and mobilizing collective action."*

I truly believe that God has given me a second chance. So with God on my side and opening doors for me I am pleased to walk his path. After all, my life is in His hands and one day I will return to Him as well.

I know that at times I fall into a state of ungratefulness, especially when I experience a reaction. Whenever this happens I always try to remind myself that where I am today is a far better place than where I was three years ago, or even six months ago for that matter. The fact is that there are others out there in situations far worse than my own, and I pray that God gives me the opportunity to help people who are less fortunate than me. I pray that I can continue to be grateful for situations no matter how painful my suffering may be. Having a stomachache, a headache, or swelling of the throat and tongue, is far less than what some others have to deal with.

When I first thought about getting more involved with agencies and other charitable organizations, I went to an event where I heard Imran Yousuf speak. I spoke with Imran afterwards, and he mentioned that he was a board member for a few organizations, including the Olive Tree Foundation in Toronto. Seeing him as a board member at such a young age was awe inspiring, so I did my part in consulting him for his advice on joining charitable boards myself. He was very pleased with my inquiry and gave me a number of websites and references on where to begin. Since our initial conversation, I have joined a number of boards as a board member, the first being the York Region Food Network (thanks Imran).

"And they feed, for the love of Allah, the indigent, the orphan, and the captive." QUR'AN, CHAPTER 76, VERSE 8 *(076.008)*

Having learnt the importance of food, I got involved with the York Region Food Network to help end poverty and hunger in the York Region. Because of my food allergies, I was unable to eat certain foods, but there are people out there who can eat, and want to eat, but they can't afford to. I recently had the opportunity to join the Maytree Foundation's Leaders for Change program, which helps emerging leaders learn about poverty and the various initiatives that are being considered. Some of these include youth empowerment, hunger, affordable housing, homelessness, and many more.

Empowering Muslim women

In April of 2007, my best friend Sanjitha Ranjan and I came to the conclusion that something had to be done to address the concerns of South Asian women dealing with depression and trauma, especially as a result of physical, emotional and sexual abuse. At first we were gung-ho about the idea of taking our efforts overseas, but with more and more research we came to the conclusion that there was a need for these services locally as well. This evening discussion began another project which kept us working hard for two to three nights per week. Our project was well received by many other social service agencies, and we are currently working on building partnerships with many existing organizations to ensure that proper outreach and support can be provided to all South Asian women and girls in Canada. Our organization is called Way to Inner Peace (WiP), and we have a mandate to establish a women's helpline for South Asian women dealing with abuse and trauma— specifically emotional, physical and sexual abuse and/ or violence. I can certainly relate to the gap that exists in the Muslim community and its beliefs about such issues, as well as the lack of accessible treatment, because my own life is a small example of this.

We are launching a series of women's empower-ment workshops called "From Women to Heroines." The intention is to empower women and give them an opportunity to disclose and seek the assistance they need to move on. This book is an effort to encourage these conversations by sharing my personal story.

Muslimah–Women's Empowerment & Development Organization

Today, I do my best to support Muslimah (Muslim women), and Sawfiyyah Kasozi, the "Amira" (Chair) of the Organization, has done an amazing job bringing out younger girls and giving them the opportunity to get involved and make a difference. Sawfiyyah has been an amazing friend to me as well, and we've worked together on a number of projects, including the Reviving the Islamic Spirit Conference.

Building capacity in the Muslim community

The Ontario Human Services Network is a coalition group that I helped found which really came together by what I call a ripple effect. In January 2008, after the death of Aqsa Parvez, a girl who was allegedly strangled by her father for not wearing the hijab, I felt this was a death caused as a result of domestic abuse and violence. Her father was a taxi driver who recently immigrated to Canada, and the murder occurred as a result of low income, parent–child conflict and integration issues. A few months prior to Aqsa's death, the Network had decided it was time for the Muslim community to take a stand on certain issues. We had scheduled a strategy session with the Muslim community simply to discuss the concerns and the resources available to build capacity within the community. Unfortunately, due to the weather we had to cancel this session, but after Aqsa's death I was determined to do two things:

(1) Confirm for the media that the issue was not that of the hijab, but rather that of domestic abuse and settlement issues which led to her murder. Unfortunately, the first statement released in the media was that it was a religious killing because of a conflict between the daughter and father on the issue

of wearing the hijab. This was taken from a conversation with one of her friends and from postings on Facebook.

(2) To reschedule the community strategy session to discuss how to prevent such issues from occurring in the future.

Being as frustrated as I was, I emailed a few of the more active female leaders in the community asking them to take a stand on this issue. I suggested we unify ourselves not as community leaders, professionals or representatives of different groups, but as concerned Muslim women so that a press release could be sent out to the media expressing our concerns. We held a memorial vigil for Aqsa and we were surrounded by media, with more than fifty journalists present. We made it onto every major news station in the city, and in the media interviews I promised that I would do something to make a difference and would work on the issues that were being questioned.

The second aspect that I wanted to cover was the strategy session and formation of a collaboration of Muslim organizations to battle domestic abuse and multiple community issues. The main agenda areas were on the status of women, youth settlement issues, parent–child conflict troubles, settlement for new immigrants, and poverty issues for families.

To do this, we conducted the strategy session with

the help of several of my friends: Saleha, Rabia, Shaila, Urz, Rubina, Samia, Hajar, Zahida, Amira, Maryam D, Rifat, and others. The session turned out to be a well-attended event, and with thirty of the top religious and non-profit leaders present we were able to come up with concrete issues that we would work on. Since then, we formed a steering committee and are working on a number of issues through collaboration.

In a way, I'm grateful to my father for allowing me to carry on his legacy. He began the first mosque in Mississauga and put down the foundation of the religious community in our city. Now, I'm striving to do the same in order to build the foundation for the Muslim social services sector. However, I can't do this alone, and knowing that I have friends that are willing to go the extra mile to make a difference is all the more promising. I guess because of my father, people at least give me a chance to speak.

The importance of finding good mentors

> *"One of the sweetest, sincerest and most generous joys of life comes from being happy over the good fortune of others."* ROBERT HEINLEIN

As I discovered from childhood, mentorship is probably the most important thing you can have. It's important to surround yourself with peers, but always remember to keep others that are more accomplished in your circle as well. You'll be surprised how quickly doors can open when you know the right people. I remember being at an event when someone asked me how I knew all the speakers. If only people knew that many of them were my mentors, whether they believe it or not (Doug, Imran M, Saleha, Amanuel M—thank you all).

Summit for Leadership & Social Responsibility

I decided to put together CAMP Toronto's first Leadership Summit. The Summit was a large event held at the Markham Civic Centre with a capacity of four hundred people, and included over thirty speakers. All of the speakers were qualified and experienced professionals who were there to share their experiences and successes with other people in order to inspire them to become leaders one day. The event was a lot of work, but it was definitely a great initiative to take CAMP Toronto to the next level. Through this experience I met many amazing people who have really inspired me to continue doing the work that I'm doing. It's nice to know that so many people are supporting this initiative.

One of these people is Dr. Muhammad Benayoune. There were many great things Dr. Benayoune told me as we sat and discussed community issues over a number of meetings, but there was one particular point that really resonated with me. He said Allah* has infinite wealth. If everyone was granted their desires, then the amount of wealth that would be used from His vast treasures would be like dipping a needle into an ocean and taking it out. This is from a hadith (prophetic tradition). Hadith Qudsi 17:

> "O My servants, were the first of you and the last of you, the human of you and the jinn of you to rise up in one place and make a request of Me, and were I to give everyone what he requested, that would not decrease what I have, any more that a needle decreases the sea if put into it."

Dr. Benayoune also said God is the most generous, and when you do something generous He will always accelerate and extend the generosity to make it far better than you had ever imagined.

Another speaker at the Summit was Uzma Shakir—a Pakistani Muslim woman (formerly a new immigrant) who has changed the face of the social service sector for women and newcomers in Toronto. She's done amazing work and is truly an inspiration to many. I remember her speaking about leadership and the importance of commitment versus contribution. When you're a leader, you make a commitment;

and the example she used to demonstrate this point was absolutely amazing: A chicken and a pig are walking down the street and they see a sign at the local restaurant window that reads, "Eggs and Ham $1.99." The chicken looks at the pig and says, "Let's go inside, this looks like a great deal." The pig turns to the chicken and says, "Wait, I have to think about this—for you it's a contribution, but for me it's a commitment."

At this time, I was invited to join the CITY Leaders program. The program was being piloted by United Way of Greater Toronto, The University of Toronto, and the City of Toronto. It's a program that takes the top twenty-six youth activists and leaders and walks them through how to be a leader in the not-for-profit sector. I was very humbled when I was told that I was one of these twenty-six (also known as "Renaissance 26").

Through this process I met a number of amazing people, and the first person that helped me get to a new tomorrow was Mawuli Chai. He would be the fifth angel to appear in my life since my journey began, and it's by no coincidence that his name means "There is a god." Getting to know my new non-Muslim friend Mawuli was certainly rewarding.

Face your fears

On the first night of the CITY Leaders program retreat, Mawuli started telling me how impressed he
was by me and the positive aura he felt from me. He
was very pleased to meet me and had a feeling that
I am destined for something very big. He also said
that it was destiny that brought us together for a purpose. He was right. When I left that night, little did
he know that I was still quite terrified of him—if not
emotionally, certainly physically.

The next day during class he made a point of
coming to me and asking me how I was. In the
evening, he came to me once more and asked me
how I was doing. I'm sure he could tell I was visibly
upset, so he took me aside and asked me how I was
honestly feeling. I looked at him and said candidly,
"I told you I was no longer hesitant, but the reality is that I still am." His immediate reaction was,
"Don't tell me, he looked like me didn't he?" I was
speechless, but he was right. He responded by saying,
"But mama, I didn't do it. It wasn't me." I nodded
and said I know, but it's still hard and I'm sorry. He
looked at me with genuine concern and asked how
we could fix this. He thought for a moment and then
said, "You and I will need to spend as much time
together as possible," and with that he grabbed my
hand and held it for most of the evening. I know that

this would be considered an incorrect act in my faith, but in all honesty, it was something I needed. Had he not reached out and held my hand, I probably would still be afraid beyond belief as a result of an incident that happened over seven years ago.

At first, I was so terrified I couldn't even think to move his arm away. All of the memories I had hidden so deeply suddenly surfaced. I closed my eyes and started reciting my prayers to Allah* to help me out of this. Then after almost one hour, I felt at ease and my body stopped shaking internally and I started to feel my breathing slow down again. He looked at me and said, "Farheen, you and I are here for a reason, and God brought you to me. It's destiny. You needed to meet me this weekend and I hope that I've helped you." When I got home that night, I truly felt free, like I had a huge burden lifted from my shoulders. I finally felt that I could just be me, not having to worry about covering myself with makeup to feel the part, or to wear multiple layers to feel secure enough to walk among people. I finally felt like Farheen, the once carefree loving person that I was whose purpose in life is to spread the "happiness" that I am named after. Now when I close my eyes, that face that has haunted me for so long is finally replaced by my dear friend.

Looking back, I realize now that it was almost as though my friendship with Mawuli was planned; as if

I needed to prepare myself before running into him (the perpetrator) once again. Life can be so scripted, and we as human beings often don't realize these things until we look at them from an outsider's perspective. After many years of struggling to suppress the incident that occurred, I never thought I'd see the day when I would see the man who attacked me once again. But life made us meet eight years later when I was visiting my doctor's office, which is directly across the street from *the* building.

I saw him standing in front of the bus stop outside my doctor's office. You could say that chance brought us in front of one another, but for me it was destiny. In a way, it finally gave me the opportunity to get the justice and closure that I needed to move on; something I had been longing to have for so long. Luckily, he didn't recognize me, which gave me the courage to walk away as quickly as possible. I can't imagine how I could have reacted if he did see me. The moment I saw him, I was consumed with the same feeling of helplessness that I felt that day. I was terrified that he'd find out who I was or remember me, and somehow I managed to drive myself home from the doctor's office. All along the twenty-minute car drive, I recited Qur'anic verses trying to keep myself as calm as possible. When I got home, I didn't know what to do.

The worst part was that, not only did the memory

of that day come back, but so did the sensations of touch and the emotions that went along with it. At first I didn't know what to do. I went into my room, turned off the lights, turned on music loud enough so no one could hear my sobs. Then I sat on my bed shivering from fear that he would somehow find me. A feeling of self-disgust came over me and I was furious at myself for feeling this fear. The only thing I could think of was, what could I do right there and then to make this feeling go away? I prayed to God to give me an answer. After trying to keep myself together and trying to think hard, the only thing I could think of was to open up my computer and to go onto Facebook to see the faces of some of my closest friends who would help me feel present and safe.

I tried to stay strong in front of my folks, but the moment I made eye contact with my mom the tears started to flow. I wish I had the strength to keep her out of it. The worst part was that my dad was there to listen and was very angered at the whole situation. His comment was, "It's in the past, forget about it." I know he meant well, but it's easier said than done. That night, my father took the day off and sat with me trying to console me, telling me that I was a strong girl—a "patan" (a strong tribe in India that we originate from) who could handle anything. I was a leader, doing so many wonderful things. Why should I feel ashamed or guilty for something someone else did?

Being a leader wasn't the problem, it was the feeling of helplessness that really brought me down. I felt useless and completely incapable of doing anything at that point. At first I didn't know what to do. When I spoke to my grand uncle, a retired staff sergeant with the police force, he told me I am a champion and a trailblazer, and that he knows I can make it through.

Seeking help

Whenever you're reliving an experience, remind yourself that you're in the present and not the past. Be prepared physically, emotionally and mentally to move on.

After an initial attempt, I never did go for formal counselling, and I decided that my work, my life and my writing are all a form of healing. I truly understand the importance of seeking help in whatever way you feel comfortable doing, and I did speak to many people including my family doctor. Generally, opinion was divided, and some said I should continue working on my recovery myself, and others said I should seek professional help.

As part of seeking my own recovery, I met Brother Ibrahim Downey. He is an amazing person who has been helping people in jails find themselves and return to a good life. Brother Ibrahim helps people understand the beauty of connecting to God and our higher purpose in life. A friend of mine suggested that I speak to him about my problem. When I told him about the incident, he sat me down one afternoon to enlighten me about a way of approaching life. He told me to imagine a box to store away the incident. Learn from it what you can and then store it away, so that you don't have to keep remembering it. He then asked me if I wanted to be above the line or below the line. Even though I wasn't sure what that meant, something told me that I should be above the line. He asked me the question again, "Do you want to be above the line or below the line?" So I repeated that I wanted to be above the line in a place where I could learn to come out of the issues that I'm facing.

LEARN
BLAME

If you are in a position to *learn*, than you have the opportunity to *earn*. Similarly, if you're below the line, then you're in a position to blame others, and so essentially you're lame.

He said the most important belief a Muslim has is Taqwa (belief in God or God consciousness), and there are three main aspects that affect a person: Love, fear and hope.

- Love is affected by external communications (something that others often control/affect by their actions).
- Hope is technical knowledge of how to keep things in balance.
- Fear and internal communications are things you can control from the inside.

All of these aspects can be either positive or negative, and for the most part we have control over what they are and how they affect us. He continued by saying that if any one of these aspects become more powerful than Taqwa, then there's an imbalance and a problem. So what does that mean exactly? It means that if I love someone or something more than God, or I fear something more than God, or I hope or have faith in something other than in God, then I have a problem. That really put it into perspective for me, and I questioned whether this fear I was facing was stronger than the fear I had for God. I think not! Nothing is more important in my life than the presence, faith and belief in Allah*. You can replace this model with whatever you feel is the point of your existence, and it still works the same way.

Brother Ibrahim shared many interesting mnemonics with me:

Help	**F**ollow
Other	**O**ne
People	**C**ourse
Excel	**U**ntil
	Successful

Seeking justice, finally!

A close friend of mine suggested I speak to the authorities and to a counsellor. I was a bit hesitant about sharing my feelings with someone else, but after a little while I finally decided to give it a shot. I called the local assault crisis line and got a very disturbing response. Being South Asian, I told the lady that eight years ago I had an attempted sexual attack and I didn't tell the authorities. Her immediate response was, "Oh, well what makes you think your parents won't disagree with you calling us now?" I called back again to speak to another lady hoping to get a better response, and she started the conversation asking if I felt suicidal, adding, "You must be afraid he'll find you, right?" Neither of these two thoughts had crossed my mind, and because I was somewhat in control I didn't fall into that dark place based on her comments—but others may have! Needless to say, that attempt at counselling didn't go well. At that moment, I decided to get involved with that organization to help them with racialized and cultural education. I am now on their board of directors.

The next step was to tell the authorities. I refused to call and tell them, even though my mom was insistent that I do. The reality was that at this point in time there would be no evidence to charge the perpetrator, but that for my own well-being and for closure I should still make the report. So I did. It was probably the most uncomfortable feeling that I've had—sitting in a room with a female officer while describing each and every moment, movement and action that took place.

Abaya: Empowering yourself

I started to realize the elegance of the abaya once again. For years, I had refused to wear it because it reminded me of the incident. Allah*, why did I wait so long? Seeing it hanging on my door each and every day for the last four years, I never once thought to try it on until this moment. Thank you God for reminding me that an abaya is more than just a cloak. It's something that gives you the privacy you need, but at the same time, it's a way to express yourself without having to be measured by the standards set by society. Wow, I can see myself wearing it more often, and who knows, maybe someday I will wear it daily like I did years ago before my journey began. As Muslim women, we can choose to be covered and no man has the right to take that away from us. Sometimes, it's okay to let loose, but the choice should be ours and ours alone. Now I realize that I can make that choice. By not wearing it, I was giving him the power and now it's time to take it back.

Leadership in the community

Recently, as I was driving along the 401 Highway in the fall, watching the rows of coloured trees lined up painting the landscape like a vibrant rainbow, I realized just how beautiful the world around me is. We all have opportunities to see the beauty in ourselves and others but we often don't take the time to see the beauty of creation. It also reminded me that Allah* is the Creator who sustains all of this, and that in the grand scheme of things I'm just a microscopic creature in comparison to the vastness of this world. We think that as human beings we do such amazing things and put ourselves on a pedestal for it. But who are we really? Let's put this into perspective. The second thing I have come to terms with is the fact that my life's goals have changed so drastically. In a positive way, nonetheless, but it's a complete 180 degree flip in terms of what I wanted and where I'm headed towards now. In the past, I was focused on becoming a top-level executive at one of the big banks, with a huge house on Mississauga Road and a Mercedes. I was working towards an MBA and ultimately focused on the possibility to earn money for my own future and the future of my family.

My goal now is to build capacity in the community by establishing social enterprises and agencies that will help people on a day-to-day basis. It's all about youth empowerment, women's rights and newcomer settlement facilities to help them integrate into society, as they rightfully should. And even more importantly, my goal is to work in the community to develop a positive image for Muslims, to help eradicate the issue of Islamophobia that affected my life and many others. Being persecuted for something someone else did is unacceptable, and we can't stand on the sidelines anymore and watch while others behave differently with us. Like Dr. Tariq Ramadan once said in one of his lectures that I attended at Waterloo: "There's an 'us' versus 'them' mentality, and human rights violations will continue while this attitude exists." So, our job is to become a part of the larger community and be seen as Canadians so that when injustice occurs, everyone speaks out and not just the minority Muslim community. To do this, we need to develop our own leadership.

Leadership is ultimately the ability to influence change by being a part of it, rather than trying to push it onto others. We were all witness to Barack Obama's presidential campaign motto: "Be the change that you want to see in the world." Well, this statement actually came from Mahatma Gandhi, who also used it to affect positive change in the world. I'm sure we all have a place in this community that we can call our own; a place where we can contribute and make a difference.

Once I started becoming more active in the community, my family (especially my father) started to have issues with me working for the community, working late, and probably the most important element—becoming more involved in community service rather than working in the corporate sector. After a while, it got to me and I didn't know how to react to it. One night when it became unbearable, I prayed to Allah* for an answer as to whether I was doing the right thing. That night I dreamt that I was standing in a white hijab and abaya and I saw a man in a white ihram (white robe worn in Mecca). The man is the Prophet Muhammad[†]. He comes towards me and hands me an envelope. He looks me in the eye and says, "Farheen, you have everything you need to succeed in your life. Good luck!" I couldn't believe it. The Prophet himself came to me and since then I never doubted the work I do. I know that as long as my intentions are in the right place, it's all good.

> "When we stand for nothing, we fall for every-thing." MALCOLM X

I recently joined a leadership program through the Maytree Foundation called *Leaders for Change*. It's focused specifically on the eradication of poverty in the city, and begins with a two-day retreat where we were asked to do several team-building activities on self-reflection to truly understand ourselves as a leader. One of these activities was to develop a personal mission statement. When I first wrote mine, I thought it was something out of a superhero movie, but then I realized that each and every one of us has the potential to become a superhero in our own way. Okay, maybe not a superhero, but a hero nonetheless. Here's what I came up with:

> "To live life knowing that each day is a gift and that life is a precious commodity that we will be held

accountable for. Remembering that life's purpose is to please the "Almighty" by remembering him in both joy and hardship, and by making a difference in people's lives everyday. Using my talents, knowledge and creativity, I will come up with creative, ambitious solutions to empower and mobilize people, communities and humanity as a whole in order to ultimately end world poverty and hunger; while looking for talent and potential in others, to empower them to take on a leadership role and the responsibility of creating a brighter future."

This program is very different from the CITY Leaders program in that I wasn't as experienced as the others in the room. I kept very quiet and tried my best to learn from the questions being asked. I remember one person coming up to me and saying: "Farheen, I just want you to know that even though you don't say anything in the room, you still have this twinkle in your eye, as though you're going to change the world, and that helps me feel grounded, so thank you for that."

Going through training programs is great. It equips you with the tools necessary to make the changes you want to see in the world. I know that as a result of my challenges I have not had an opportunity to complete my undergraduate degree, but I will do so in time. Learning is a part of my faith, and Muslims are told to do whatever it takes to seek knowledge, even if that means travelling to China and back. In my mind, I am continually learning, maybe not in the conventional sense, but I'm learning nonetheless. I have friends like Asma Bala and Sameena Eidoo that are working on amazing things like their PhDs in religion and in education; which is phenomenal. Being able to create your own research and putting something into the world which you call truly yours must be amazing. In their own way, they too are changing the world, but through their thoughts and their words. So like I said, no matter how you do it, it's definitely possible.

Uzma's example of the chicken and the pig is classic; and so the question is will you make a contribution or a commitment? How will you achieve it? And what do you need to do to get started? With Allah's* help, I have now found the courage and the ability to move forward and start a completely new chapter and pave a new road. A road where everything is foreign but one where I know I'll get more signs and meet more people as I walk on the path of righteousness for the betterment of people everywhere. Let's see where destiny takes me now. I know what I have to do, but it's how it will take place and what the outcomes will be that will be interesting to see.

Despite all of the crazy things I've been through

over the last few months, especially while writing the end of this book, I also had to look for another job. I decided that rather than beginning a new job, I would just focus on consulting on a full-time basis, which by the grace of God Almighty is working. My fundraising firm is called FSK Associates. The FSK, of course, stands for "Farheen Shabana Khan."

Through this business, I have had a chance to help many small organizations develop solutions for funding, and also have the opportunity to educate people on the methods of fundraising and how they can make a larger impact with the right infrastructure and processes in place. Of course, I still have a lot to learn, but life is a learning process, right? I still remember my first client, Nadia Aslam, who helped me land my first contract. From client to friend, Nadia has played an important role in helping me overcome some of my hesitations as a new business owner, but more importantly, some of the serious obstacles in my life as well (thanks Nadia for being there. You're awesome!).

I'm now at a point where I think I may need to clone myself to get all the work done, but it's all good. It's interesting to see people's faces when they ask me what I do and I tell them I'm a consultant. It's a lot of fun helping people see their potential in the non-profit sector. The most exciting part of this new endeavour is the role I just took with United Way of Peel as the Community Outreach Coordinator. I work directly with the South Asian Advisory Council and upper management on how to better support and service the South Asian community and engage them in United Way. I am honoured to have been given this opportunity, and look forward to working with them for many months to come. My allergies are now 95 percent cured, and although I still experience some bodily swelling, headaches, aches and pains and lethargy, it's become a part of who I am. I always remind myself that life has challenges, but it's these challenges that make us who we are.

In the long run, there's a lot to do and very little time. I really don't know where I'll end up. Some people say I should run for city councillor in the next municipal election, and others say I should become the CEO of United Way in five years time. Only time will tell. Imam Hamid Slimi, a local scholar in Toronto, said to me, "You don't have to be the way you are Farheen, but you chose to be that way." That's definitely true, but I've only been able to do that through the guidance and the signs that God has provided.

Coming to the end of this book made me realize that this is just the beginning for me living as a new me, in a new life, with the promise of a new tomorrow. It's said that success is 15 percent knowledge and 85 percent attitude, and I completely agree. Like a wise owl once said, "The future belongs to

those who believe in the beauty of their dreams."
I'm ready to start a new chapter in my life, are you?
Who knows, maybe down the road we'll meet again
... only time will tell.

Don't wait. Pursue your dreams today!

There's a popular Hindi/Urdu proverb:

"Kal karey so aaj kar, aaj karey so abhi."

*"What you planned on doing tomorrow, do today,
and what you plan on doing today, do now!"*

Good luck!

*"May God give you: For every storm a rainbow, for
every tear a smile, for every care a promise and a
blessing in each trial. For every problem life sends,
a faithful friend to share, for every sigh a sweet song
and an answer for each prayer."* IRISH QUOTE

In Summary

- Life is like a book. Each chapter is created with a lot of thought and care.

- When one chapter ends, the next one begins.

- As the chapters progress, you continue to follow along;

- but the final chapter is a mystery until the very end.

- Always keep in mind that...

- Life is full of challenges, but its how we deal with them that makes us who we are.

- No matter what the challenge, there is always a way out.

- All you have to do is see the light and walk towards it.

- Make the intention and watch the pieces fall in place.

Sincerely,

Farheen Khan
www.farheenkhan.ca

Acknowledgements

First and foremost, I would like to thank Allah* for giving me the opportunity to write this book and share my story. I know that I could not have written this book without the encouragement and support of my family and friends.

My father was very skeptical of my allergies, but he's a very visual learner. After the carrot sweet episode he made a point of trying to understand and did his best to be there with me at doctor's appointments and other tests I had to undergo. He prayed to Allah* to take all of the blessings he had earned from his work at the mosque, and use them to make me better. Thanks Baba, I really appreciate that.

My mother was there with me from day one. She was there when I licked the first spoon of soy pudding, and when I experienced my first anaphylactic shock. She has stood by me on every moment of my journey. My mom did her best to keep the peace in the house, which at times was difficult because others sometimes forgot to wash their dishes after eating something I was allergic to, tie the garbage, or open the windows.

My elder sister Sabena did her best to make me feel welcomed in her house, but it was tough, especially when other guests were over. She tried her best to cook in such a way that would allow me to stay. Thanks Badeapa for trying to help me feel welcome.

My sister Afreen was working at a grocery store and would always bring things home for me to eat. She would walk the aisles in search of things that would make me smile. Thanks Afreen. You're the best.

My sister Ayesha always tried to keep me motivated and explain to me that there was more to life than food. Thanks for your wisdom Ayesha. I may not always take your advice, but I definitely appreciate the time and effort you put into trying to convince me.

My brothers Shoaib and Muzammil probably had the hardest time not eating any junk food at home. Everything manufactured is made with vegetable oil, which I was allergic to, and they would stand outside in the freezing cold to eat samosas, cookies and pizza. Thanks guys, sorry for all the trouble.

My kid sister Maryam, and my roommate of a number of years, saw how difficult it was for me to stay positive, so she would do little things to make it better, like making a plate full of shredded cabbage and tomato paste thinking it was an alternative to spaghetti. Thank you Mary.

My nieces Juwi and Summi were such sweethearts through it all. They made me little crafts. And Juweria, or "sugar" as I call her, would call me up on a daily basis to see how I was tolerating foods and smells. It was definitely a joy to have the two of them with me when I needed their support. Thank you babies, love you both.

I thank my grandparents for their prayers, and my Grand Uncle Jamal Khan for his inspiring words. Thanks to Nazim Chacha and Roma Chachi for believing in me when others lost hope.

Uncle Jameel always applauds and encourages me for the work I'm doing in the community. He reminds me to keep a work–life balance. My Grand Auntie Phuphuma gave me the courage to live life as an independent woman, and my Uncle Saif Mamu was always trying to make me feel comfortable around others so I didn't have to feel like the alien or outcast just because of my allergies. My cousins Parveen and Sophie Bahiji both helped and inspired me to make a change in my life for the better. Thanks ladies.

When I got close to the 95 percent cure mark, my friend Yusra re-introduced me back into the social world of eating at restaurants.

May Allah* grant my late uncle Laiq Chacha— Jannah inshallah (paradise, God willing). He always listened to all of my crazy ideas and encouraged me to pursue my dreams.

My "aunties" Shahida and Rashida may as well be my blood relatives. Thank you for your support, prayers and kind words.

My best friend Sanjitha ("Jitha") Ranjan is my shoulder and my confidant. In our seventeen years of friendship we have shared everything with one another. Jitha is a Hindu-Tamil woman and I am a practicing visible Muslim. Yes, we got strange looks, and we still do, but we have learnt to appreciate our differences.

Some of the important people on my journey have been mentioned throughout the book, but I will say that each and everyone who helped me get through my trials and tribulations are near and dear to my heart. You have all made an impression on me, whether you realize it or not. Please know that I will always be here to support you in whatever you do.

About the Author

Farheen Khan is a consultant in the non profit sector. Her clients currently include United Way of Peel and the North American Spiritual Revival (NASR). She is a community activist and sits on many voluntary boards and committees. She lives in Toronto, Canada.